AYAHUASCA
MOTHER OF REBIRTH

Get updates at:

http://Journeying.ca

"Shamanism is an old growth forest, cut down by lust for lumber and power. But the roots are resilient and deep, the seeds endure the biting cold and the wind. We rise to face the sun again, guided by the whispers of the ancients."
~Ankhara

Table of Contents

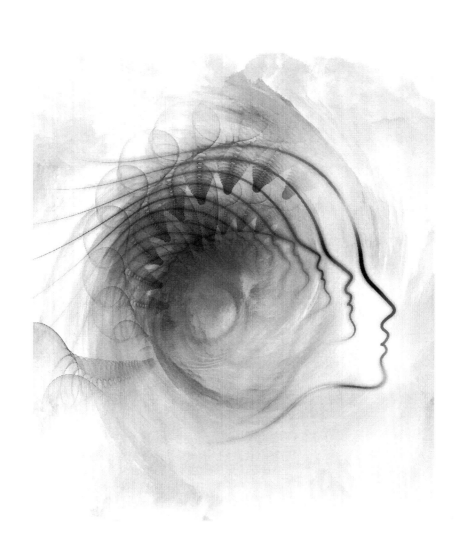

Part I: AMoR

The intention of this book is to share wisdom with you relating to Ayahuasca and shamanism, to support you on your path of healing and spiritual inquiry.

This book is not a recommendation to drink Ayahuasca– far from it. What I am offering you is a deeper understanding of the potential benefits and risks of working with Ayahuasca, *within the broader context of shamanism as a whole.*

I mentioned Ayahuasca to an acquaintance once. He jumped up and exclaimed, "Oh, careful with that! *That stuff will change your life!*" And so I say the same to you: if you choose to have a meeting with Ayahuasca, you will never be the same person again. Don't take that lightly!

An Ayahuasca ceremony is not a "trip", nor a recreational experience. I suggest you put it in the same category as getting a large tattoo or having surgery because of its powerful and lasting effects.

That doesn't mean you should be afraid, but to be honest most of us who work with Ayahuasca, even after years, feel anxiety going into a ceremony. Why? Because the ego fears change, fears losing its power over you, fears you seeing the veil that's been pulled over your eyes... But, more on that later.

Some of the things I will share with you are considered secrets.

Some teachings are secret because they can be dangerous to the spiritually uninitiated, and so they will remain sealed away in the realm of the esoteric (that which can only be taught through experience or initiation). Everything I share with you is intended to expand and clarify your understanding, to help you make more harmonious and informed choices.

I humbly offer my interpretation of what I have learned and continue to learn from my ancestors, teachers, and elders, the first of which being my Táltos grandmother. This book is not "the truth", simply the understandings I have come to after years spent immersed in spiritual teachings and practice. I have witnessed my own healing and evolution, as well as the healing of my tribe, and I hope that what I share with you will lead you to the *"breaking of the shell that encloses your understanding."*

There can be some confusion about names and Ayahuasca; there is the Ayahuasca vine, the Ayahuasca brew, and the spirit of Ayahuasca. For the sake of clarity, I will call the vine "the vine", the brew "Ayahuasca", and the spirit "Abuelita". I will cover the nature of the vine, practices involving the brew, and the mysteries involved in working with the spirit.

There is currently a tremendous surge in interest about everything related to Ayahuasca. This signals a positive change in the direction of humanity.

Ayahuasca is awakening seekers and showing us a way to lead a more harmonious existence on Earth, helping to break down the traumas which fester in the soul. These deep pains which prevent us from connecting and engaging with ourselves, our bodies, and our environment are ripe for remediation. Abuelita guides us toward profound healing by reminding us of who we are, by revealing the seat of our essence.

If you are an aspiring seeker on a spiritual path, someone who is hungry for self-knowledge and spiritual wisdom, or if you're curious and seeking for a path, welcome.

If you are a thrill seeker looking for your next high, please ask yourself, *"Why does my life feel empty and meaningless when I'm not filling it up? Why do I feel the need to stuff the void with adrenaline fixes and uninterrupted stimulation? Why can't I just **BE**?"*

People who are drawn to Abuelita looking for their next thrill end up getting much more than they bargained for*, a direct spiritual experience, or at least a direct experience of their deeper hidden selves.

We fill up an emptiness inside because we're seeking *something*. Abuelita helps reconnect us with that missing *something*, which is ultimately **the Self**.

If you've been running through the emotional desolation of the modern world all your life, you may react to the thought of connecting with a hidden part of yourself with cynicism.

Your cynicism and doubt are understandable and well founded; look at the world you were born into: a world where deep connections, deep thoughts, and deep truths are becoming rarer by the moment, where all beings are measured against their value as units of production and standardization, where absolutely everything is commodified, and where power is ceaselessly concentrated and centralized.

Pacifiers are handed out at every turn; comfort is seen as the highest aim.

So no, I am not offended in the least if you are cynical or skeptical; in fact, it means you are an uncommonly thoughtful human.
The revelations which flow from shamanic journeying – the knowledge that everything which you thought you knew was only a childish illusion – is terrifying.

You want to believe that you are a member of an advanced civilization, somehow special, chosen. Yet the further you look in, and the further you look out, the more you are compelled to accept how tiny you are in the vastness of space.

The teachings of Ayahuasca help us not only to accept this condition, but to embrace it as a gift, to embrace how tiny we all are against the sky.

Have you ever considered how extraordinary it is that all of material existence is held together by a loose web of incredibly small particles? That what your brain tells you is matter is only a cluster of near-nothingness creating the illusion of a *something*? That this book, as the unified structure it appears to be, doesn't exist?

I don't share that thought with you as some **trippy psychedelic mental masturbation**, but a sincere and sober inquiry: how deeply have you contemplated the nature of being? Do you remember the sense of wonder you felt as a child as you regarded our vast, incomprehensible world?

As you read these words, you may find that there are more

questions raised than answered. If nothing else, I hope that what I am about to share will awaken the childlike awe which sleeps somewhere inside you.

Together, you and I will probe the world of the purely subjective. What's true for me might not be true for you. I can direct your attention, and suggest *where to look*, but I will not attempt to tell you *what to see*.

* You are warned that drinking Ayahuasca outside of a sacred ceremony, or in a ceremony held by an inexperienced person, can be dangerous and can lead to overwhelming experiences which the uninitiated may find damaging. In some cases, bad reactions can even be life threatening.

Abuelita teaches you to stop seeking your specialness and self-importance, and instead to live your **purpose**, and to **accept** your place in the macrocosm. To live for your highest good, for the benefit of all beings, rather than an ego-centred existence of either attempting to be the same as everyone else, or better than everyone else. Or similar enough to everyone else to be accepted while maintaining a vague yet persistent sense of superiority.

She illuminates the understanding that when you accept what you are, a tiny fragment of an enormous creation, you can find peace in that understanding, as well as your place. Your home.

When you stop running away from your past, your trauma, your body, and your planet, you can actually **experience reality**, rather than the comforting nursery illusion that has been pulled over your eyes, and which you have lapped up since birth. With that comes profound **personal power**. Once you're in touch with a more direct reality, you have all

5

the more power to *"Be the change that you wish to see in the world."*

As a society, our personal responsibility muscles are severely atrophied, and this is where Abuelita comes in. She supports us in clearing out old neural blockages, old belief systems, and old addictive habitual patterns of behaviour with her deep compassion and tenderness. With her support and kindness, she softens the pain of facing the consequences of our choices.

It's my aim to share enough with you to send you on your way with a solid footing, and with a well-rounded understanding, but truly it's all in the practice. Theory will not get you far on this path, but it may help to keep you safe and to guide you like a compass. As you go forward in AMoR, I'll share valuable techniques and practices with you. If you only *read* them and don't attempt them for yourself, *they will not help you.*

If you're already on the shamanic path and working with plant teachers, it is my hope that this wisdom will round out your knowledge and fill in gaps that get left out in modern settings.

Please understand this: **reading this book does not make you a shaman or curandero**. Right relation to these teachings means that anything you learn here is intended to be used **by you, on you, for you**.

As someone born into shamanic practice, and who has been actively walking the shamanic path for over 20 years I must tell you: once you begin walking on the spiritual path, you can never walk away from it. What you come to know about yourself, about spirit, about existence, you can never unknow. Once you've set foot on the journey of understanding the mystery, all of life becomes a spiritual experience.

Remember: if you find yourself on a path that does not urge you to take action in your daily life, question, "Is this a path that that will take me somewhere, or is this empty philosophy?"

The shamanic path is fundamentally a path of action.

Within this book are quotes from great teachers, both modern and ancient, from a broad spectrum of traditions. You may wonder, "What do the thoughts of a Taoist, or a Sufi, or a physicist have to do with shamanism?" The answer is: more than you might expect. Shamans aren't known for leaving a great deal of written material behind, while teachers from related Mystery traditions with valuable knowledge have been more verbose and generous with their prose.

Within the traditions that seek to understand and connect with the mysteries of the universe, many common themes can be found, because the subject of their search is the same: understanding existence.

As Rumi said,
"Sunlight appears different on this wall than it does on that wall, and different again on that wall there, but it is still one light."

Teachers from different traditions may speak about the Creator and Creation and use countless names from countless languages, but in they end they describe one light, one phenomenon: *the mysterious grace of life, existence, and consciousness in the manifest universe.*

If a rose by any other name would smell just as sweet, what does that say about the creative force which produces the rose, the generative and destructive forces of the universe? Do those forces care if I call them Allah, Wakan Tanka, Siwar Q'cnti, God, Shiva, or any other words capable of passing through the human mouth?

I don't think those forces are concerned with our possessive obsessions, and so within this text I use the names Creator, Great Spirit, and others interchangeably, without implying that these forces or their anthropomorphisms can be comprehended by humans in their vast totality.

With that said, while there are some fundamental similarities between diverse shamanic or animist cultures, we must keep in mind that every culture is its own. They have their own songs, their own ways, their own history and destiny. I do not aim to even scratch the surface of the anthropology of shamanism here, because the topic is too vast and diverse, though we will explore shamanism as the universal human religion of the past. I use the terms Shaman and Curandero broadly for the sake of simplified communication; the word my ancestors used is Táltos.

I will cover the concept of subtle "energy". What I mean when I say energy is being attuned to the emotional and physical sensations moving through your body and mind. Once you are aware of the sensations that move through your experience, the name becomes unimportant. What matters is the phenomenon itself; a direct experience of the subtler levels of yourself that comes only through strengthening and sensitizing your connection to the Self.

Finally, "ego" is a recurring theme here. I address the ego as the conceptual framework inside the mind which creates the thought or belief "I have a self, I am a unified self; I am a person and separate from other people and my environment." This illusory construct is rapidly dissolved in shamanic ceremony, and so working with the ego is an important element of our work.

If you're already familiar with the basics of Ayahuasca, you can skip to **Abuelita: The Spirit of Aya** on page 20.

The role of the shaman is to go to the good spirits and the ancestors and find the cure for illness, and to guide the tribe forward together along that good way. While I can't sit with every human on Earth in ceremony, it's my hope that this book will aid in reducing the illness in the human heart, and that it will guide you in a good way.

What is Ayahuasca?

Banisteriopsis Caapi: The Vine

The word Ayahuasca (pronounced ah-yah-WAH-ska) comes from the Quechua language, an ancient native language of South America, and means "Vine of souls".

Banisteriopsis Caapi is a climbing jungle liana (vine), native to South America. The primary active ingredients are harmala alkaloids, which are monoamine oxidase inhibitors (MAOIs). They allow dimethyltryptamine (DMT) to be orally active. DMT is introduced from the other primary ingredient in a traditional Ayahuasca brew, *psychotria viridis*, also called Chakruna. Without the Ayahuasca vine, the DMT is metabolized and has no effect.

Before the combination of the vine and the DMT containing admixture plants (such as *p. viridis*) was discovered, the *caapi* vine was used for its purgative, cleansing, spiritual, and hypnotic properties. It's said that the vine provides the teachings, while the admixture plants add light and colour to the teachings so that they're easier for humans to understand.

DMT naturally occurs in many plants and animals; in fact, as you read this, a substantial amount is flowing through your body. Tonight when you dream, there will be even more, as humans cannot experience dreams without DMT.

Ayahuasca: The Brew

What is it? What will I feel when I drink it? Will I throw up?

Before embarking on a journey, it's important that you ask yourself,
"Why do I want to do this? Why do I want to start a relationship with this medicine, with this plant teacher?"

Drinking Ayahuasca tea is not pleasant, comfortable, or fun by any stretch of the imagination. Although it can be deeply rewarding and life-changing, it is serious and demanding work. To experience her treasures, you will require a sober approach, a disciplined path, deep self-preparation, and space in your life for integration.

Before you set off upon this path, take the time to meditate deeply upon the answers to the above questions. *Do not be in a hurry!*

Patience is a virtue that is greatly rewarded when working with Abuelita Ayahuasca. Take the time to prepare yourself for the work, and for each journey. Take the time to integrate each experience, whether it's overwhelmingly strong, or so subtle that it seems that nothing happened.

Understand that Ayahuasca healing is an ongoing path and not something that happens instantaneously— it's not a magic bullet. With deep commitment and profound courage, a well-integrated experience with Ayahuasca can be life-transforming and elevate you to profound states of bliss and understanding.

If you find yourself protesting, "But my life is *too busy* for all that integration." Then perhaps the first step for you is looking at why you must keep yourself so busy. What's waiting for you when you stop and simply *be* with yourself? What do you experience when you sit and do nothing for five minutes? No thoughts, no actions, no plans, just sitting?

Take time to deeply consider your reasons for wanting to initiate a relationship with Ayahuasca and her fellow plant spirit teachers, as well as the intent that you bring.

Here are some quotes about this sacred sacrament:

"Yagé is many things, but pleasant isn't one of them."
~Wade Davis

*"The worse the experience, the better the payoff. There is only one requirement for this work: **You must be brave**. You'll be learning how to **save yourself**."*
~Kira Salak

"I am within the battle, suffering but I'm happy.
In it I am learning what I did not yet know."
~Santo Daime hymn

"It is an X-ray machine, not only of the health, but of the virtue, maturity, humility, and equilibrium of the person. Since very few of us are saints, the shock between what you think yourself to be and what you really are produces strong reactions... The truth is not that yajé is too strong for us, but that we are too weak for it... [It] is a battle and the field of combat is in your guts... All you have to do is to let the vine carry out its work, but without a sufficient experience... you are stuck between the nausea and your fear, which produces

12

an unbearable anguish, because it is a nightmare that seems to have no end. The evil spirits that you see in this fix, which are reflections of the battle between the true and false self, take on a life of their own, so as well as the physical pain and distress of self-recognition, you have to deal with monsters.... The feedback between [the drinker's] fear and the fire in the guts drives the suffering into a spiralling descent, a circle so vicious and dizzying that he sometimes believes it will terminate in death.... There were still times when the terror was absolute, instants of dread that I will carry to my grave."
~Jimmy Weiskopf[1]

*What makes an Ayahuasca brew "**Ayahuasca**"?*

Simply, any tea made from the Ayahuasca vine is Ayahuasca. While this may seem obvious, today some ignorant or unscrupulous people make a brew which they call Ayahuasca with either Syrian rue, which also contains most of the same alkaloids, or synthesized harmala alkaloids. Syrian rue is much less expensive than the Ayahuasca vine, but the experience is substantially different.

Syrian rue contains toxins not present in the vine, which can cause bodily harm, especially with repeated or long-term use. There's nothing necessarily "wrong" with these brews, or any other medicine you may choose to explore a relationship with, but if it's not Ayahuasca, don't call it Ayahuasca!

In addition to the vine, admixture plants are usually added, depending on the type of healing the curandero (shamanic healer) is guided to offer. Ayahuasca without any other plants is an experience of its own, though outside of the jungle it's unlikely you will find a curandero who will offer a vine-only brew.

Chakruna is the most common admixture plant, and in the eastern part of the Amazon, especially in Brazil, Chaliponga (*Diplopterys cabrerana*) is more common.

Chaliponga tends to be a stronger and more challenging brew, while at the same time being less colourful and less visual, as it also contains 5-methoxy-N,N-dimethyltryptamine (5-MeO-DMT), the more potent cousin of DMT. Those who are unprepared can find working with Chaliponga to be a profoundly difficult lesson.

The Taste

Ayahuasca is famous for its strong taste, which may be very bitter or sour. Tasting peppermint, ginger, or raspberry afterwards can cleanse the palate.

Some find the taste palatable the first time drinking, only to find it less pleasant during each following experience after they experience purging. Some see the strong taste as part of the experience, a psychologically important ordeal, the first dragon to be confronted. And some even enjoy the taste. Of course, in the jungle the taste is just accepted and taken as a given.

Some journeyers put a great deal of effort into minimizing the unpleasantness, especially in cases where the taste causes such strong nausea that participants cannot keep it down long enough to begin the journey.

In English speaking countries I've sometimes encountered a strong dogmatic emphasis on never doing anything which might distract you from the taste, as if it were a heresy laid down in an old book.

I offer this to you: do as spirit directs, with a watchful eye on the ego. Do what you need to do to find your own healing, and to forge a bond with Abuelita.

The Purge

For most people, the medicine will trigger physical purging of toxins in the body and the brain[2], correlated with purging of blocked emotions and memories, and the releasing of negative belief systems. This experience is often euphoric rather than painful, not at all like being sick with the flu.

The purge (la purga) may be strong or mild, may happen several times in one journey or may not happen at all, but it is a central part of the medicine and the overall experience.

There are ways to reduce the purge, but if you can learn to accept it and flow with it, the purge can actually be pleasurable. It's a deep release and purification. If you fight it, it becomes more difficult and unpleasant.

The best approach is to just say "*Yes, thank you.*"

Give in to it, surrender to the process, and go with her hand in hand – or head in bucket. Imagine all of the distractions, discomfort and pain you have within you released with each purge, and accept it as part of the experience.

Name whatever is coming up, such as, "*Guilt. Rage. Passive aggressiveness. Undeservingness. My mother's expectations.*"

It is after the purge that the best part of the experience often begins, where things become lighter and easier, filled with grace and beauty. In effect, you cannot travel to the higher places weighed down by lead. So leave it behind and soar on your wings!

The clearer your system is going into the ceremony, the better prepared you will be to receiving and integrating the spiritual energies and knowledge of Abuelita.

Go easy on yourself the during your experience if you feel ill-prepared. It takes time doggy paddling and treading water before you learn to deep-sea dive.

Along with the purge, Ayahuasca can have a strong "body-load", a feeling that gravity is stronger than normal.

From a modern perspective, the purge and the body load have a great benefit: they make recreational use or abuse of Ayahuasca highly unlikely, preserving her for spiritual and medicinal use.

How is Ayahuasca Prepared?

Each of the 100+ tribes that have traditionally prepared Ayahuasca have their own recipes, rituals, and practices, though fundamentally the process is similar.

They create a relationship with the vine and Abuelita over time, harvest the vine, break it up, put it in a large pot layered with the admixture leaves, add water from the Amazon which is naturally acidic, and boil for a day.

Those who are going on the journey gather, go through the rituals and spiritual preparations they are called to, as enshrined in the traditions of their tribe, and everyone drinks together, including the curandero.

Prayers, healing medicine songs called *icaros*, the smoke of wild jungle tobacco (mapacho, *nicotina rustica*), and healing intentions flow throughout both the preparation, and the internal part of the ceremony.

Unlike organized religion, nothing is set in stone in shamanic practice, even in cultures which have managed to preserve their traditional knowledge.

Everything is guided by spirit and ancestors, and so each curandero, and each group, have their own way of "being with the mystery". As outsiders, sometimes we can fall into the expectation of standardization, as it's a strong value in Western culture. However, what's being offered is far more valuable than any dogma; spirit guides the process in the same way a lighthouse guides sailors to safety.

It may be stormy and sometimes dark in a journey, but at the light-source there is unobscured clarity and brightness. The closer you are, the more time you spend in the light, and the more intense it becomes. So the aim is to have the courage required to move through the darkness, and to humbly listen to the call of spirit as it guides you home. Discerning spirit from the siren call of ego and self inflation is a never-ending practice.

Approaching a Ceremony

When approaching a group or individual working with Ayahuasca, some questions that will help you to discern if it's a good fit for you are:

"Does this resonate with me, how does this feel in my body? Do I feel safe with this person? What are their intentions? What is their training or lineage?"

You will likely feel some emotional discomfort regardless of the group. This comes naturally from within yourself whether the group is integral or not, because the work itself will stir you deeply.

In other words, check in with your baseline anxiety about facing your shadows before you meet anyone related to Ayahuasca, because you will inevitably project those fears and anxieties onto them. Then, when you do project onto them, you will be familiar enough with your inner struggles to recognize the fear and anxiety as your own, freeing you to accurately assess the reality of what's in front of you.

How should I approach the Ayahuasca ceremony?
With profound respect, gratitude, and surrender. These are protective forces that will help you align with your own healing forces, and with the macrocosmic healing forces.

Divine Feminine and Masculine

Once you know you're in a safe place, with a good shaman, surrender, and surrender again. There is a time for masculine power, and a time for feminine power, and during the ceremony is the time to let the feminine principle unfold. This means having the courage to surrender to the process and work with the medicine as a birthing mother surrenders to the birth and works with the baby, moving as one toward a profound act of love and creation.

The feminine principle is the root of all things, the great mother. She is the subtle canvas on which existence is painted; always surrendering and yet overcoming everything; permeating all things and yet made of no-thing. You harmonize yourself with her grace when you lie on your back in the river of non-action and allow her to carry you, as she has always carried you in all of your days and all of your nights. Round in her perpetual birthing, eternally open. In her incomprehensible vastness she is like water, slipping through your fingers no matter how tightly you grasp.

Excellent masculine feminine energy descrip

The masculine principle, by contrast, is that which is vertical, active, and emissive. The force inside of you which commands you to take action and participate. He is pointed and closed, defined and measurable, an arrow loosed over the horizon, a goal in pursuit, always hunting and climbing; restless.

These principles exist in all things and are accessible to all humans, regardless of gender. They are inseparable lovers tangled in the divine mystical union, the foundations of the dualistic reality which we perceive.

Abuelita: The Spirit of Aya

Madré Ayahuasca, Abuelita, Little Grandmother; what you call the spirit of Ayahuasca is not important. Any name you give her is not her true name.

She imposes no dogmas, asks for no offerings, and often hides herself. She is an ever-flowing fountain of wisdom, healing, and truth, available to all who seek her teachings with humility and purity of intention.

She does not care if you believe in her or not, only that you respect yourself, respect the teachings, and do the work. Abuelita is a diminutive form of grandmother in Spanish, and essentially means Granny, or Little Grandmother.

Each experience, each sitting with Abuelita is unique. It's different for every person and it's different every time we come to learn her teachings. At times the experience can be mild, and seem as though not much is happening.

At other times it can be so intense and overwhelming that it feels as though your entire being is exploding and dissolving as it's shot from a cannon through the universe at the speed of thought. This is her way of teaching, and you must learn to surrender, accept, and say, "*Yes, thank you*" to whatever she's showing you.

Abuelita has no need for worshippers. It is as if you and I are worms lying on a sidewalk after a heavy rain, and she is a passerby generous enough to pick us up and place us back on the grass. What can a worm hope to offer the hand that transports it to refuge? Nothing.

20

The greatest thanks we can offer is living a strong and healthy life to the best of our ability, to aim to live in harmony and integrity with all that is.

This also reflects **Ayni** (*right relationship* or *reciprocity* in Quechua) with Mother Earth. We have nothing to offer her, no way we can improve her, other than with our love and respect. She offers us the chance to live in beauty and harmony if we are wise enough to accept, though as we are coming to understand the offer is not unconditional and our place here is not guaranteed.

We don't ask the cells in our body to worship us, and don't hear them if they do. We ask that they serve their purpose to the best that they can, at the order of magnitude where they exist, and that they not become cancerous.

I don't think it's a coincidence that Ayahuasca may cure cancer in the human body[3], while turning the human being away from disharmonious thoughts and actions, making them less cancerous to the Earth.

Again, I remind you that there's no need to place a negative meaning or judgment on being tiny, in the same way that there's nothing wrong with a toddler who's learning to walk and falling down. They're just small, and one day they'll be bigger and more experienced, more dynamic. Even though we are tiny, we are a hologram of the entire universe. Within each microcosm of the human being, exists a blueprint for the macrocosm – the whole of creation.

In the shamanic animist worldview absolutely everything, from humans to helicopters, is embodied with and animated by spirit. With a tender heart, and a relaxed mind, we interact with the beneficial spirits of the world and learn all that they have to teach.

Humans have a gift for waking up those spirits. When you call upon a loving spirit to work with you and offer them your thanks, you're engaging in the work of bringing our species back into harmony.

Abuelita is here to help you purge your own sickness, and therefore become less sickening; to help you no longer be an agent of illness. We can only speculate as to how Pachamama's cells, which are so young on the cosmic scale, contracted such a pernicious cancer.

"Ancient things arise from one:
The sky is whole and empty.
The earth is whole and firm.
The spirit is whole and strong.
The 10,000 things are whole and alive.
All these are in virtue of wholeness.

When man interferes with the Way,
the sky becomes filthy,
the earth becomes depleted,
the equilibrium shatters.

Therefore, nobility is rooted in humility;
loftiness is based on lowliness.
The pieces of a chariot are useless
unless they work in accordance with the whole.

One's life brings nothing
unless lived in accordance with the whole universe.
Playing one's part in accordance with the universe

is true humility.

Truly, too much honour means no honour.
It is not wise to shine like jade and
resound like stone chimes."
~Lao Tzu, 39th verse Tao Te Ching

Remember that Abuelita is just a gatekeeper. You are introduced to her through the material of the plant, and she opens a door to wherever and whenever you need to go, for your healing and the healing of the planet.

It's important to not become fixated on her, on seeing or experiencing her. As the Zen master Linji said, "If you meet the Buddha, kill him." Otherwise, you might sit with him (or the dazzling illusion of him) forever and never move toward your own enlightenment.

What matters most is that you take what you learn, take what you experience, and apply it personally to your life. After you've experienced her teachings, use them to be more kind and forgiving to yourself, more accountable to your thoughts, actions, and choices. Then, through deep reflection and personal change, you will have known her on a deep level.

Healing Effects

Why do humans drink Ayahuasca? The fundamental answer is simple: we're imbalanced and we want healing and harmony. Since ancient times, the relationship with Abuelita has supported those who work with her in regaining and maintaining that state of balance.

Some of the healing is direct, catalyzed by the purgative and strongly cleansing effect of the plants, and what appears to be an ability to fight cancer in ongoing in vitro research.

Ayahuasca flushes out receptor sites in the brain[2], which is helpful for all ailments of the mind, especially hard drug addiction. But the deeper healing comes from the effects that the medicine and the ritual have on the emotions, mind, and soul.

Ayahuasca supports you in facing your darkest shadows, your most repressed traumas, and your most serious wounds. What if you could return to your childhood and relive your darkest experiences with your current strength and maturity? What if you could give yourself all of the love you never received? All of the nurturing, holding, and tenderness that every child deserves?

This is what Ayahuasca offers in a deeply real and experiential way. I'm not talking about taking a stroll down memory lane; it's possible to experience past events as if you were really going back in time. How would your life have turned out differently if someone had stood up for you, and been a warrior and protector for you?

You may say, "All of that stuff that happened to me... that built character." And it probably did. But along with character comes a hardening of the heart, and in some cases mental illness.

That *character* teaches you to repress your needs, repress your natural guidance which comes from your body and soul, to become deaf to your deeper needs. It forms the *false personality* [4], the mask that's worn to cover and protect your true inner Self from a world that is callous and hurtful.

Through painful experiences, you built coping mechanisms, behaviours that reduce stress and generate a sense of normalcy. And until the **underlying wound** is healed, until the causal emotions are faced and integrated, the part of you which experienced trauma and found a way to cope with it continues to run the same program over and over, endlessly. A gaping hole remains, and you try to fill it with whatever is at hand while life feels like a prison. [5]

Age has nothing to do with it. If you experienced trauma at three, that part of you is still three, and it will not age until you go back to stand up for him or her.

Time, unfortunately, does not heal all wounds. Time numbs wounds, teaches you to normalize or ignore your dysfunctional behaviour, and gives your wounds time to fester and leak out into your life while the suffering part is crying out, "Heal me!" constantly. [6]

Over time, running away from pain leads to more and more painful experiences, all of which can be interpreted as your inner healer saying to you, "Turn around and face it!" But, without support and guidance, the simple act of stopping and facing the shadows that haunt you is unthinkable.

Fortunately, not everyone experiences major trauma in childhood, though statistically many do. Reported rates of verbal, physical, and sexual abuse paint a grim picture, and those are just the cases that are reported.

It should come as no surprise that Ayahuasca is currently being tested in clinical trials for treatment of post traumatic stress disorder (PTSD), as well as with First Nations people who experienced serious trauma in the "care" of the residential school system, and with people who suffer from serious addiction, which is almost always rooted in childhood trauma.

Whatever is not working in your life, right now, in this very moment, I can say this with certainty: you will find the roots of it in your childhood regardless of whether or not you can remember the moment that the seed was planted. Children do not have the capacity to process and integrate traumatic events in the same way adults do, and so the trauma affects a child's whole being in a deep and reality-bending way. Trauma causes internal changes that extend from the limbic system, to the way the brain stores and retrieves memories, to the child's expectations of life in adulthood.

A cultural maxim exists that says, "Something's not working here... let's make it look better." but this is like chopping down a holly tree over and over. If you cut down a holly tree this year, next year you'll discover a holly grove in its place. If you focus on the appearance, asking, "How will this look to others? What will they think of me?" and ignore what's going on inside, or worse, pretend that "inside" doesn't exist, the roots of what you **don't want** go deep, and wide, and spring up in every inconvenient place. The pernicious roots serve an important purpose from the perspective of the false personality: to keep you stuck, bound, and clinging to familiarity.

Imagine if professional sprinters had to run on a track covered with enormous binding roots. How fast, and how far could they run? Your essence is like this. It's ready in every single moment to give you a life more fulfilling than your wildest expectations, but there is too much undergrowth between you and Spirit.

When the roots are ignored, or covered over with cement, true freedom, true liberation, is simply unattainable. I don't offer this to you as a dogma which you must accept, but as a sincere offering from my experience, and the experience of the hundreds of seekers that I have worked with. Since *what you resist persists*, at some point you must find the courage to dig deep; if not now, when?

A major factor for healing which is also a psychological risk is Abuelita's ability to give space for repressed memories to surface, which can be viewed as deeply buried, rotting, tangled roots of trauma.

This process can be demolishing for individuals that believed they had made it through childhood unscathed, a person who might be heard to say, "Oh yeah, my childhood was normal. Average." Sadly, normal and average are nothing to be proud of. In the words of Krishnamurti, "*It is no measure of health to be well adjusted to a profoundly sick society.*"

In the surfacing of memories, one's life can potentially be destabilized as the identity crumbles; the mind says, "That's it. No more. I'm taking a break to deal with this." And business as usual grinds to a halt as one is forced to face, or desperately avoid, what has surfaced from the basement of the psyche.

And, troublingly, the memories that surface are not always literal, or clear. They can be only flashes, or fragments, or sensory memory, or, most challenging of all, factually incorrect.[7]

In the case of a surfaced memory, seeking professional help immediately is strongly recommended, with a therapist that is trained to support one through this kind of experience.

Seeing a therapist that is poorly trained in this area can result in them unintentionally planting false memories, since the mind is looking for something to hang on to. While this only happens to a very small number of people, it's important that you're prepared for the possibility of it happening to you. For an artful portrayal of the process of revealing, falling apart, and healing, I recommend seeing the film *Bliss* (1997).

Aside from a catastrophic dissolution of the identity, it's more likely that the identity will be intensely challenged. This is a healthy process, where some of the very deepest work occurs. Imagine you've had a map, which you've called reality, that you drew when you were four years old. Do you remember how well you were able to draw as a four year old? Well that's your map, but you don't call it that.
You call it, "**The truth.**" or just, *"The way things are."*

In ceremony, as ego attachment loosens you may come to realize that, *The map is not the territory.*

You are presented with the chance to erase, burn, redraw, and otherwise correct the map, not just from your perspective as an adult but from the perspective of higher wisdom, higher guidance.

A second risk is the possible surfacing of mental illness. Ayahuasca and entheogens in general do not cause any type of lasting psychosis. The mechanism isn't there[8]. However, they can trigger psychosis, schizophrenia, or other serious mental illness which has previously been buried, asymptomatic, or otherwise manageable.

It's important to understand that this is healing trying to happen. There is no space in the dominant culture for people with mental illness to heal, because the culture itself is conducive to mental illness. More often than not, individuals experiencing psychosis end up heavily sedated and don't receive the care they need, the care which is perhaps their birthright.

In the case of structural damage to the brain, or in any case where the brain is somehow neuroatypical, I recommend taking a great deal of time for research before considering participating in a ceremony. With that said, Ayahuasca and other plant medicines have been shown to increase neuroplasticity.[9] Ayahuasca may help the brain to form new pathways, and become more functional in the process.

If you came through childhood with more subtle wounding, or have had the courage to grab a shovel and start digging yourself out of the shit, Ayahuasca offers you the chance to connect with your higher and lower selves, with your essence, and with your purpose.

In a quiet moment, have you ever wondered, *"Why am I here? Why am I on this planet at this time?"*

While Abuelita may not serve you the answers on a silver platter, she offers the space, the tools, and the compassion to explore these vulnerable existential questions.

Is Ayahuasca a Shortcut?

A shortcut implies that you are in one place and you want to get to another, and you *know where you're going*.

Imagining for a moment that human experience has defined levels, have you experienced your life at the next level? How about your life 10 levels up? If not, then a shortcut is a potentially precarious path to take! You cut through the woods because you think you'll get home faster, fearful because the sun is going down; maybe you'll get home faster, maybe not at all.

In my experience, Ayahuasca work is closer to a guided tour than a shortcut. Abuelita opens a door inside of you and invites you to walk through. She extends her hand to yours, wants to show you the mysteries of yourself and the universe. But do you accept? Or are you blinded by the light, sprinting aimlessly through the galactic wilderness?

Inside of the guided tour, you are shown everything you need to see in rapid succession, spurring an *evolution* inside of you. She takes you behind the scenes through the inner door, but it's not any *shorter*, just *faster*.

At some point you may come to believe that you *must* go behind the scenes to do inner work, that it's pointless to walk alone when you can sprint with her at your side, and that's when Ayahuasca becomes a distraction rather than a tool. A spiritual crutch.

Parts of your subconscious are still infantile because the dominant culture lacks rites of passage, and because trauma stunts emotional development. Abuelita will catch you up with yourself, and then the rest is up to you. If you explore on your own, you will find that you can achieve extraordinary states of well-being and consciousness without her and without any other plant teacher. If you don't believe me, perform the Air Element ritual in Part II and you will never doubt your ability to traverse the spirit realm unaided again.

So many of us are still infants inside, fused with our mothers and wanting someone to nurse us so we can feel those golden melting feelings of merging and divine union.[10]

Abuelita will love you, hold you, and nurse you, and then she will shove you out of the nest like a good mother should! If you never spread your wings and soar on your own, dissolved into the wind and showered with grace, *what is the point?*

So come and nurse, if your heart feels bereft of connection and full of pain. Abuelita is here for you, modelling the cosmic mother that you crave. Once you've relieved yourself of your burden and filled up on divine milk and unconditional love, remember that the whole point of life is to grow and become a self-actualized adult.

No, **Ayahuasca work is not a shortcut**. It's a profound vehicle that moves at the speed of thought, with Abuelita at the wheel. If you get out of the vehicle and are content to spiritually bypass your inner work, I say this to you lovingly: don't expect to get anywhere worth going.

The Inner Healer

The inner healer is a voice inside of you which encourages you to become your own spiritual authority, become your own teacher, your own elder.

Rather than learning about spirituality from an external authority, this voice suggests that you do what spiritual masters do: block out all of the noise so that you can hear the ancestors and the fragment of God speaking to you from within. In this way, external teachers serve to guide you more deeply into yourself and your personal connection with Spirit and the ancestors.

Organized religions developed to put an intermediary between humans and Creator, and have diligently worked for thousands of years to maintain their supposed mediumship.

Direct spiritual experiences have been suppressed in favour of empty ritual, and today those same spiritual experiences which laid the foundations for modern religions are deemed pathological by modern medicine and dangerous or demonic by organized religion.

Someone experiencing a state of rapture, if taken to a hospital, would be called psychotic. I don't mean to imply that psychotic episodes are inherently spiritual; rather, that not all breaks from "consensual reality" are signs of illness.

The direction of the inner healer as a concept is something mysterious, and often only makes sense in retrospect. I'll take a detour here to share the story of a former addict with you, to illustrate my meaning:

"I was hooked on heroin and crack, and spent all day every day trying to get my fix. One time, I spent days lying in the dark on psychedelic mushrooms. After that, something changed in my life... I knew then that I had to get clean and start living my life."

He made a full recovery, inspired by his experiences on mushrooms, which at the time were *just another trip* to him. He wasn't consciously seeking healing.

He began public speaking, and sharing his story at schools focusing on the dangers of addiction (not the healing power of mushrooms).

He didn't know that he would have a life-changing experience; he was simply seeking short-term relief from his suffering, but something inside of him was guiding him toward an unpleasant experience that would bring about a positive change in his life.

Why do some humans become addicted to drugs? The overly simplistic answer which has been tossed around without question for almost 100 years is "drugs feel good, and they're addictive." But this narrative hasn't been supported by modern science or shamanic wisdom.

During the Vietnam War many soldiers were using heroin. Upon return to the USA very few of them ever used heroin again, despite the horrors of war that they had experienced and the wave of PTSD-induced escapism.[11]

If the addictiveness of the drug was the key, you would expect that most of the heroin users would have stayed heroin users. Instead, what's being revealed more and more, through studies of the lifelong effects of adverse childhood experiences, is the understanding that the deeper causes of addiction are a lack of connection, and changes that happen in the brain as a reaction to trauma.

Every day thousands of patients in hospitals are given diamorphine for severe pain, which is essentially strong, pure heroin. Yet addiction to diamorphine is rare once the patient has left the hospital. The drug is just the *seed;* what matters is whether the heart is torn up fertile ground where the roots of addiction can take hold in the suffering.

Coming back to the inner healer, again I ask, why do humans use drugs? From a shamanic perspective, they are using drugs because their spirit is weak, their heart is sick, their soul is scattered, and they are disconnected from their source and environment. This is the result of traumas; personal, intergenerational, cultural, and global. Humans are drawn to substances and negative behaviours to fill in the holes that these traumas leave behind.

The inner healer is a force which pushes you toward relief from suffering. Sometimes, you take a detour on the path of healing which leads you toward behaviours with short-term gain and long-term pain, as a battleground for fighting inner demons.

Ideally, the inner healer takes you toward opportunities to overcome those demons, to experience short-term pain with long-term gain, as is often experienced during shamanic rites and ordeals.

The biggest difference between drug abuse and working with sacred plants in a ceremonial way is that drugs offer short-term relief with long-term pain, while in ceremony you are confronted with the pain that has been eating you from the inside out. If you can successfully confront and release these shadows, you may get the chance to lead a more free and connected life.

The inner healer is that voice that guides you toward a painful ordeal, and encourages you to overcome it and heal something from the past. It encourages you to react differently than you would in the past, or to not react at all. This isn't to say that spiritual teachers are irrelevant or without meaningful guidance, simply that your inner healer knows more than anyone else about what *you* need to be a better version of yourself.

As Kahlil Gibran said in *The Prophet*,

"Your pain is the breaking of the shell that encloses your understanding.

Even as the stone of the fruit must break, that its heart may stand in the sun, so must you know pain.
And could you keep your heart in wonder at the daily miracles of your life, your pain would not seem less wondrous than your joy;

And you would accept the seasons of your heart, even as you have always accepted the seasons that pass over your fields.

And you would watch with serenity through the winters of your grief.

Much of your pain is self-chosen.
It is the bitter potion by which the physician within you

heals your sick self.

Therefore trust the physician, and drink his remedy in silence and tranquillity:
For his hand, though heavy and hard, is guided by the tender hand of the Unseen,
And the cup he brings, though it burn your lips, has been fashioned of the clay which the Potter has moistened with His own sacred tears."

If you find yourself wondering, "Is this the inner healer, or the ego?" know that the ego will speak in absolutes, it will try to keep you stuck in familiar routines, and it will try to prove the negative voices in your head right. The inner healer nudges you toward experiences that are bitter medicine, without punishing you or judging you. You can ask yourself, "If I listen to this voice, will it keep me in the same loops which no longer serve me, or is it possible that it will lead me to a new stage in my evolution?"

Journeying Realms

Each person experiences the journey in a completely unique way, and no two journeys are exactly the same.

However, there are some "realms" that are commonly visited. Here they are defined in linear terms; in the experience, beyond the mind, they are more ephemeral and flowing. I share these with you simply as inspiring thoughts, not as a map or something to aspire towards.

The Biological

- Going inside of your body, exploring areas that are constricted, blocked, or ill, exploring movement of energy through the body.
- Getting more deeply connected to your body, and reconnecting with parts of yourself that you have felt shame or guilt around.
- Reconnecting to parts of the body that you have dissociated from.
-

This can sometimes be a painful experience, where you feel the trauma which you've been running away from; all the pain which has been repressed, ignored, and normalized. I cover this in depth in Part II.

It can also include going back to the causal events and emotions which generated the pain, and releasing them from the root.

The Biographical

- Exploring and healing one's life, identity, and traumas.
- Visiting with friends and family members, deceased and living, to settle anything which needs to be resolved in the relationship.
- Connecting with ancestors, and receiving guidance from them.
- Much personal healing is available in the biographical realm, and the teachings from this realm are some of the easiest to apply to daily life.

Deep personal healing takes place here, with the ability to go into past experiences, and charge them with positive healing energy, to take your younger self out of traumatic situations and place them in protection, to "fight the demons" of your past, or to forgive them.

You are presented with the opportunity to speak what you never had the words to say, to hear the apologies you always deserved to hear, and to see people from the past for who they truly were: imperfect, wounded humans, doing their best without tools, healthy models, or support.

The Lower World

- Exploring the instinctual qualities of yourself.
- Can be a dark and swampy experience since much dysfunction is stored and processed here.
- The realm of the snake. The mind struggles to enter this instinctual realm, and you may feel that you're losing your sanity.
- Contains your most raw authentic self.

Lower world experiences can be deeply integrative.
Here you can reclaim parts of yourself that have been cut off and abandoned. This can be called a soul retrieval; the detached parts of yourself are found and brought back into yourself, into your wholeness. From a young age you're taught to reject the deeper instinctual parts of yourself because your environment doesn't support them, but they are still a part of you.

For example, a rambunctious and physical child that is forced to study and take tests from an inappropriately tender age might come to believe that they need to be still in class to receive love and validation. So they cut off their life-loving self, because they instinctually know "Without love I will die!" And so a false personality is built over top of the part of their essence which was rejected in favour of survival. In the lower world, you can reconnect with this essence, making the false personality unnecessary.

Work can be done with ancestral spirits carrying unresolved issues from their life, or who aren't aware that they are deceased and have not moved on. This passage, called psychopomp work, is especially powerful if the deceased is a close relative and if you are able to offer them forgiveness and love.

This place is also where vitality, creativity, imagination, playfulness, and a connection to your inner child can be reclaimed.

This is a place where negative influences can be extracted, cleansed, and released. Cords or attachments to people, places, or things which no longer serve you can be severed.

The Middle World

- Confronting your conditioning.
- The shadow realm of the masks you wear to function in society, a place where the myriad ways you've compromised yourself to gain approval and validation are laid bare.
- The realm of the puma.

This is often a challenging experience as what you are exploring is the world you live in, except seeing it for what it is with all of the truth and ugliness exposed.

You may see how the wool has been pulled over your eyes, and your view of the world, of "reality" may never be the same. After these experiences, it's common to be less susceptible to advertising, and to be less tolerant of old paradigm values such as hoarding, concentration of power, mass consumption, shirking of personal responsibility, and addictive comfort-seeking behaviour.

It's also common for dietary habits to change, and often results in reducing or eliminating consumption of meat, drugs, and alcohol. This is the level where you're looking microscopically and with brutal honesty at your behaviour and choices, seeing the effects on yourself, your life, and those you care about.

The middle world can also include a state which I call "circuit-overload", where a mental pathway, usually one related to an obsession in your daily life, becomes highly charged with energy, and an intense thought loop occurs. The same pathway is explored over and over, until it collapses and you are free from the obsession.

The Upper World

- Connecting with higher beings, with your higher self, with beneficial spirits and guides.
- Seeing your infinite power of choice in every moment.
- The realm of the condor.

This is where you may have the best results from asking for protection and guidance, to be shown what you've been blind to, and to get an elevated perspective.

This is the realm where you want to focus your prayers and requests for help, because the beings here are intensely powerful and will ask you for nothing in return. It's not a transaction; it's a blessing of unconditional love.

Asking lower spirits for help often results in needing to bargain or trade. They are not much higher than you in the spiritual hierarchy, and they may ask for things in return in the same way another human would, or lead you down a detour.

When asking the higher beings for help, they will not ask for anything in return. What could you possibly offer them?

If you are asking a spirit for help, the only thing you should offer is your acceptance, receptivity to being helped, gratitude, and a commitment to using their blessings in a good way. If they suggest a course of action, you decide whether or not it's right for you.

The Trans-Personal

This includes a broad spectrum of experiences, all of which go beyond your ego self; a broad perspective which transcends your individual self.

- The mythical and archetypal.
- Experiences of the Divine, and of deities.
- Directly experiencing the collective unconscious.
- Experiencing birth, and the basic perinatal matrices as described by Stanislav Grof.
- "Shapeshifting", changing into a plant, animal, or other element of the natural world and exploring their perspective.
- Viewing scenes from the past, sometimes including past life experiences.
- Visiting other planets, learning with the beings there. This is well established in the traditional work with Ayahuasca.
- Experiencing realms of pure sacred geometry.
- A "lighthouse" experience, where you are merged with the infinite grace of everything. In this place, you see what awaits you if you live your life in a better way, bridging the gap between personal and transpersonal.

The Group-Mind

This means having a shared experience of journeying with the the rest of the group, and experiencing the same or similar elements along the way.

When in ceremony as a group, it's common to connect spiritually with others on the journey and to aid each other in healing. During this experience, for example, you may notice that you feel a strong need to purge but can't. Then someone else purges, you feel relieved, and you notice that what you were holding on to was released.

Interestingly, when first discovered in 1915, an alkaloid in banisteriopsis caapi was named *telepathine* because of the demonstrable telepathic abilities gained while drinking the medicine; it was later realized that telepathine was already known as harmine. These telepathic abilities included being able to go into a journey as a tribe, experience what was happening in that inner realm, and then individually relate it afterward.

This "map" is intended to spark your curiosity. It doesn't cover the truly infinite landscape of unique places that can be experienced while working with Abuelita Ayahuasca. These are the foundational places, places ripe for deep healing. There is an opinion that it's better to leave the process of exploration entirely up to the one going on the journey, and there is wisdom in that, simply because knowing the map may give you the misunderstanding that you will be able to direct your experience.

For example, someone who is uncomfortable in their human incarnation may read the list I just shared and say, "*Ooooooooohhh*, I want to visit another planet!"

So they find a curandero and participate in an Ayahuasca ceremony, only to be disappointed because they spent the whole time in agony, processing a lifetime of deeply repressed pain and abandonment.

That experience would be a blessing, and exactly what they needed since the repressed pain was resulting in their lack of grounding, which equated to a life where they could gain no traction in anything at all, whether mundane or spiritual.

Hopefully you see how this knowledge is a double-edged sword: you may have an idea of where it's *possible* to go, but that doesn't mean you can control where you *will* go or *should* go!

When working with Abuelita, you must surrender to her wisdom, and to the wisdom of your inner healer. The practice lies in **fully embracing every experience you receive**, whether subtle, sublime, or hellish. Sometimes you must go through hell to get to heaven.

It is a fundamental principle of this work that there are no "bad" experiences, only challenging ones. And the challenging ones are the most likely to improve your life. Why? Because they are taking you where you absolutely need to go for your healing, deep into your shadows where you have been afraid to tread. The divine holds your hand, while you confront the bullies of your childhood.

What if I took the medicine with the intention of connecting w/ others?

Navigating Through a Difficult Experience

The phrase, *"Yes, thank you."* followed by a deep cleansing breath goes a long way to having a more manageable experience.

Remember that if you are finding an experience difficult, this is when healing is happening on the deepest levels. Ask for help! Pray. Focus on your intention while in the journey, especially if you're deep inside. Remember that whatever you are being shown is exactly what you need to be seeing right now, whether it's painful or pleasurable to experience.

Breathe, ask your spirit guides for help, ask Abuelita for help, ask Great Spirit for help, ask the curandero for help, ask your ancestors for help, and do your best to stay inside your experience for maximum healing effects.

It can be valuable during a painful or difficult experience to be held in a tender way, to be cradled like a child. Comfort is generally opposite to what one will experience in a traditional Amazonian ceremony, which tends to be completely hands off.

Cultural relevance is an important concept here: if you weren't raised in the Amazon and don't have ancestors from the Amazon, is the Amazonian approach the one which is of the greatest benefit to you?

Smelling lavender or frankincense essential oils and calling on the spirits of those plants can be valuable. Having sage or mapacho smoke blown over your body, with hands, breath, or feathers, is protective and cleansing. Sage clears negative influences, while mapacho lends spiritual strength; in fact, some traditions see mapacho as the strongest of all masculine plant spirits, which is why humans become addicted to his power.

Most importantly, ask the shaman for help, while knowing that they may encourage you to "go it alone" while they communicate with the spirits.

A trained shaman will know how to help you overcome darkness and they will negotiate with the spirits. Make sure the person you are journeying with is trustworthy before you join them through a dark night of the soul.

Any reasonably intelligent person can brew Ayahuasca tea, but only someone who truly knows the spirit realm can help you when you're in the darkest shadows.

Making sure you have the best conditions going into the ceremony means you're less likely to have an unmanageable or traumatic journey.

Dieta

In the Amazonian traditions, the process of preparing for a meeting with Abuelita is called Dieta. In this section, we'll cover the practice of Dieta, the preparation process we undertake before a ceremony. If you're already planning on attending a ceremony in the near future, this information can help you greatly. If not, **you may want to skip it for now and return to it if it becomes practically relevant to you**.

Dieta centres on avoiding specific foods, cleansing the body, keeping stimulus low, and being reflective. Every group, and every curandero has their own dieta, which ranges from borderline fasting, to avoiding only a small number of foods and activities, to the more complete vegetalista method of meditating in a hut in the jungle and drinking only the juices or teas of teacher plants for days or weeks.

Whatever the source, the intention of the dieta is essentially the same: creating space for the medicine to do its work, and preparing the temple of your body to receive a powerful spirit.

Outside of the Amazonian traditions other plant spirit medicine traditions also have guidelines for cleansing the body and mind, both before and after the ceremony; it is universally understood that to gain the greatest healing from plant teachers, and to have the clearest experience, you must first become as clean as you can in preparation. Staying clean afterwards allows the process to integrate more deeply, and to continue the inner work, and of course, to improve physical, emotional, and mental health.

48

Ultimately, each element of the dieta is up to you, whether you decide to practice it or not, with the exception of activities which could compromise your safety during the ceremony (which are explained below). I'll outline some practices, and while you read them please remember that what you do with your body is your responsibility.

Dieta is not about taking on more, as dominant culture is already great at piling expectations up to chin height. It's about taking on less – less toxins, less thinking, less mental and spiritual pollution – to create space for what's to come.

Practising dieta builds, and requires, discipline and willpower. So my recommendation is this: put in the best effort that you are able to, and do it for yourself, because you truly deserve it. In any areas that you don't meet the level you had intended for yourself, forgive yourself and let it go. The dominant culture is fond of self-torture and mental mutilation, and there's no value in falling into it. Self-judgment, stressing, and perfectionism are not appropriate here.

The dieta is intended to be followed for one week (or more) before and after the ceremony, and for as long as you choose after that. There are four areas we're concerned with:
- **Food**
- **Cleansing**
- **Stimulus**
- **Reflection**

These areas correspond to the levels of your being; your physicality, emotionality, mentality, and spirituality.

Clearing internal space and "staying light" creates room for emotions that need to come up to be felt and integrated, and exposes tendencies toward stuffing emotions down with food or covering them up with drama and other negative stress-reducing behaviours and coping mechanisms.

Eating differently and altering your routine creates reminders that you're preparing for something significant, and gives you opportunities to observe yourself, your patterns, and your reactions.

Staying light also "thins the veil", and makes you more receptive to spiritual experiences; how many prophets and monks have had spiritual breakthroughs while fasting and sitting in the mountains, or in the desert?

Physically, staying light reduces the risk of having an unpleasant reaction. Tannic acid is found in many heavy, processed, and old (especially fermented) foods. Combined with the medicine, tannic acid can cause headaches and other discomforts.

Your mental setting going into the ceremony, and the quality of your thoughts and emotions also impacts the direction of your experience significantly.

Everything that is included in the dieta will have strong positive health benefits for most people, and can be practised indefinitely if it suits you. Of course, all that I'm providing is information, and you must be the judge of whether or not something works for your system. Keep in mind that the ego looks at things that are different as being dangerous, and will do everything it can to keep you comfortable, numb, and stuck, because that's what's kept you alive until this point.

Discernment is required when asking the question, "Does this not work for me, or is it just challenging and makes me uncomfortable?" The best way of answering it is to try on the practice being suggested, and see what the effects are; to take a scientific and more objective approach, rather than relying on watery, transitory emotional states and reactions.

For every moment that you feel discomfort, every moment that you use willpower to not eat something you would love to, every time you use your neti pot, every time you extract yourself from a drama, you can acknowledge, *"**Each moment I feel discomfort is a moment I am healing and growing**."*

Food

It's important to stay away from anything processed or refined (this is key), old, fermented, or heavy, and stick to food that is somewhat bland, and as much as possible eat certified organic or homegrown. Wheat products should be reduced or eliminated, as should salt, sugar, and spices. The blandness of the dieta sensitizes the system in preparation for the medicine.

Exactly what you eat is up to you; every human body has different needs. Sticking mostly to fresh fruit, vegetables, juices, and easily digested grains is preferable in general.

The idea is not to starve or deprive yourself, but to take in foods that are simple and truly nourishing. Good examples include quinoa, buckwheat, and brown rice, sushi (without sauces, mayo, etc), and dishes made with lentils or beans, especially when soaked or sprouted. Avoid spicing, and avoid meat, especially red meat. Also reduce or eliminate foods high in sugar, "natural" or otherwise.

You're aiming for food that is healthful, but not especially interesting. Avoiding fermented foods is especially important, as they contain compounds which can interfere chemically with the medicine and cause severe headaches.

A more exhaustive "safety list" is included later in this section.

Refraining from pharmaceuticals, recreational drugs, and alcohol is an ***absolute must*** during the dieta, **for your safety**. Please take this **very seriously, as people have died from bad reactions between drugs and Ayahuasca.**

It's critically important that you disclose any herbal remedies or pharmaceuticals that you have been taking in the weeks leading up to the ceremony, as even seemingly benign or common herbs and over-the-counter drugs can cause dangerously strong negative reactions.
I cannot stress the importance of this enough, as any combinations entail a very real **physical** safety risk.

While you eat your food, take a moment to imagine where it came from: the person who stocked it at the store, how it got to the store, the person who harvested it, the plant that grew it... how it was rooted in the ground, watered by the rain, warmed by the sun, and blown by the wind. How the night sky watched over it and bathed it in starlight, on this ball flying through space at 26,000+ kilometres per hour, in an arm of the Milky Way Galaxy, held in the grace of the cosmic consciousness that dreamed it into being... As you think about its journey to your plate, thank each element involved.

Cleansing

The cleansing routine that follows takes about 10 minutes, performed first thing in the morning. It's simple, requiring in essence only water and salt, and some concentration. In terms of the salt used, look for a high-quality type such as pink Himalayan salts. Fine is preferable over coarse.

The origins of these techniques lie in Ayurveda. How does Ayurveda correspond to the work with Abuelita, and with modern Western life?

Amazonian shamanic practice and Ayurveda were both developed in the jungle, and Ayurveda had a specific purpose in its inception: to re-harmonize those who were leaving the simple life of the jungle behind to form small villages and agrarian societies.

The transition from hunter-gatherer jungle living to agrarian village living had profound negative health effects, and Ayurveda aimed to remedy them.

The techniques employed in the Amazon differ from the Ayurvedic techniques that follow in their details, in that they use fresh plants which are impossible to obtain outside of the jungle, but in terms of their intended purpose it is exactly the same: cleaning out accumulated waste from the body, which has become increasingly valuable as globalization has brought toxic products deeper and deeper into Amazonian cultures and into all of our lives.

The Amazon dieta has the deeper intention of connecting with the plant teachers as you fast and drink their juices, while our dieta will serve to cleanse your body, mind, and energy systems to prepare for Abuelita.

In addition to preparing you for the ceremony, each of these techniques has strong health benefits, achieved by reducing the toxin load in the body, and therefore the stress on all systems of the body.

The five daily cleansing activities that follow are cleansing the tongue, the mouth, the eyes, the nasal cavity, and finally oil pulling. They can feel strange or uncomfortable at first; after a couple of days it becomes much easier, and the immediate positive effects, such as easier breathing and clearer thinking to name a couple, make many people who attempt the cleanses continue to do them indefinitely.

There are some tools which make the techniques easier: a tongue scraper, a neti pot, and an eye wash cup. A good neti pot is hard to imitate, and since you can get them affordably almost everywhere, I recommend that you purchase one. As someone who practices these cleanses daily, it's my opinion that finding all three tools is worth it, and all can be purchased online. Tools should be rinsed before and after use.

Cleansing Practices

Begin with the tongue, scraping it from back to front first thing in the morning, observing what was released by the body overnight and rinsing it down the sink. Repeat until the tongue is clean, which should take less than 30 seconds.

Now take some sea salt on a fingertip, and begin to rub it into your gums and teeth. The salt creates osmosis, and pulls toxins out through the mucous membranes of the mouth.

Continue until all the gums are coated with salt, and optionally leave the salt on until the other cleanses are complete. Then rinse the salt out.

Next, fill the eye wash cup to the brim with body temperature clean water (no salt). Place your closed eye in the cup, open it, and blink a few times, then remove your eye and wipe away the water with a dry cloth. Repeat two more times per eye. Once your eyes are accustomed to the practice, you can make it more effective by doing a figure eight with the eye while open in the water.

Now use the neti pot to cleanse the nasal cavity. Fill the neti with warm water, approximately body temperature, add a pinch or two of salt, and stir or shake to dissolve the salt. The precise amount of salt generally recommended is 1/2 teaspoon salt per 250ml water.

Too little or too much salt will cause discomfort, so experiment and see what works for you. While in front of a sink, put the spout in the left nostril, tilt your head to the side, and allow about half of the water in the pot to flow through your nasal cavity. Then allow the sinuses to drain for a few moments, gently blow your nose into the sink, and repeat on the other side.

The water coming out of the open nostril can be directed with your hand or caught with a towel, or drained into the sink. Once you are comfortable with the technique, you may increase to a full neti pot per nostril.

After the salt rub, tongue scrape, eye wash, and neti pot are done, it's time for oil pulling. Place one tablespoon of organic, extra-virgin coconut oil in your mouth (either liquid or solid). Swish the oil around your mouth for 15-20 minutes, then spit out.

Within Ayurveda, a great many health benefits have been attributed to these quick and easy techniques.

Once during the week leading up to the ceremony, ideally the morning one day before the ceremony (not the day of), it's valuable to do an enema with a kit at home, or to see a colon hydrotherapist.

If you're squeamish about your body and its functions, this is a perfect chance to get more comfortable with your humanity. For an even better Ayurvedic digestive flush, search online for Shanka Prakshalana.

Stimulus

Dieta is about more than what you put into or take out of your body, it's also what you bring into your cognitive experience of life. For example, eating well and then watching Constantly Negative News is counterproductive, because you're polluting the heart and the mind.

Dieta also includes staying away from external conflict wherever appropriate, to give quiet space for internal conflicts to be heard. To facilitate this, you can ask yourself, "Is this personal? Is this about me? How can I forgive this person? How can I forgive myself? Do I need to engage with this? Is this serving me? How can I approach this situation with compassion and loving detachment?"

It's important to avoid engaging in any activity that

substantially stimulates you or alters your consciousness, including alcohol, marijuana, chocolate, tobacco, sexual activity, and also the mental preoccupation or obsession with any of them.

You're exposing the sharp edges that these activities soften. While I'm not a proponent of an ascetic lifestyle, **reducing the pleasures of life for a while gives your system a chance to re-balance**, and for areas requiring healing to become prominent.

Pleasurable stimulants tend to activate the Water element within you, making you more passive and pliable, and reducing your willpower and discipline. (*In general, stimulants are extremely dangerous to mix with Ayahuasca.*) This is in opposition to the intentions of this work, where you intend to guide your life in a more healthful, purposeful, and integral way. To balance masculine and feminine qualities, build Fire and Air elements within yourself in preparation for the ceremony, then surrender to Water and Earth when the time comes.

Reflection

"He who knows others is wise;
he who knows himself is enlightened."
~Lao Tzu

Ideally, I would suggest that you sit in a location in nature for the duration of the dieta, to be alone with your body, emotions, thoughts, and spirit. Even today, this is done in many cultures around the world as a means for connecting with self, and with Spirit.

If the thought of taking that kind of time and space is little more than a romantic fantasy for you, it may lead you to reflect on the culture and lifestyle in which you choose to live.

It's valuable to sit, rest your soul, eat little, do less, and in the process of stillness and emptiness, create sacred space inside yourself. Spending as much time as possible in nature, observing the natural world and its dance, awakens our ancient roots.

Meditation of any style, journaling, breathwork, time in nature, prayer, therapy/counselling, free association, reading quality books on inner growth and spirituality, sensory deprivation, and other practices which draw your attention inside, are of great value in preparation for the ceremony, and for understanding your experience after you've had it.

In terms of a specific practice, here is a journaling technique:

Keep your journal next to your bed. First thing in the morning, while you're still "between worlds", write a stream of consciousness in your journal beginning with "I feel..." Don't concern yourself with grammar, spelling, or anything linguistic. Focus on expressing your current emotional state, as subtle or overt as it might be.

You can jump around and write whatever pops into your awareness, however seemingly unrelated. Try to write a couple of pages as an exercise, even if what's coming doesn't feel especially expressive. If you had a memorable dream, or if a memory surfaces, you may write about it.

Then, at night, as the last thing you do before falling asleep

while in bed, repeat the process, starting with, "I am..."
practising this will help to open your subconscious, and
loosen up material to be processed during the ceremony.

Dieta and Safety

Pharmaceuticals

Interaction with pharmaceuticals can be much more
dangerous than food interactions. Even some over-the-
counter pharmaceuticals like antihistamines, decongestants,
ephedrine and pseudo-ephedrine, diet pills, and allergy
medication can have potentially *deadly* interaction with the
medicine. The same is true for **herbal medicines;** just
because they are herbal doesn't mean they're safe to mix!

For your safety, *it is critically important that you
disclose any medications or herbal remedies that you've
been taking within the last month.* When in doubt,
always talk to the space holder of the ceremony. I have
personally witnessed bad interactions with pharmaceuticals
in a ceremony held by another shaman, and it is not pretty.

The worst case scenario for a reaction with food is a bad
headache. In simple terms, you'll be fine if you stick to meals
prepared from whole, fresh ingredients. As soon as you add
packaged ingredients such as sauces and pastes, you're more
likely to get a headache.

Here is a more detailed list of foods adapted from the
American Dietetic Association and Ayahuasca.com. By
avoiding the following, you should have no problem
preventing a negative reaction with the reversible MAOIs in
Ayahuasca:

- **Anything which comes out of a package or wrapper precooked, or has more than one ingredient.**
- Unfresh, or in any way cured or preserved meat.
- Anything fermented, such as bean products (tempeh, soy sauce, miso, etc.), cheese, sauerkraut and other pickled foods, or alcoholic beverages.
- Anything containing yeast or yeast extract including sourdough bread. Breads other than sourdough and homemade bread are generally safe.
- Any soup that you did not make from scratch.
- Fruits that are bruised or overripe including bananas and avocados.
- Dried or dehydrated fruits.
- Dairy products that are close to expiration.
- Caffeine. Green tea is generally considered safe in small amounts.

For dieta I recommend avoiding these things for one to two weeks or more before and after a ceremony. For the sake of safety, 48 hours is sufficient.

Practising every element of the dieta is a large undertaking; I encourage you to do as much as you have the capacity for. *I cannot stress enough how critically important it is to follow the guidelines on safety.*

Mystical Union with Abuelita

Let's explore some groups who work with Ayahuasca. The underlying theme is one I've stated before: there's no right or wrong way of working with her, as long as she's approached with integrity. What matters most is putting forward healing intentions and cultivating a loving and respectful relationship with Abuelita and the spirits.

Those that work with Ayahuasca and other sacred plant teachers work toward personal and societal healing, and to connect with Spirit/God/Creator. This unifying intention of human healing and divine connection is key.

The examples which follow are intended to point you in the direction of further reading if the subject interests you, rather than to provide a great depth of knowledge which is only a quick search away.

There are many approaches to shamanic practice; I have been in ceremony with hereditary shamans from unbroken lines, revivalist traditions, syncretic shamans, transpersonal psychologists, psychedelic therapists, and New Age shamans. Each one of these styles have their own strengths and weaknesses, points of clarity and blind spots, illuminations and shadows. These are the approaches I'll cover here.

Historical and Modern Indigenous Use

Ayahuasca is known to be used in at least 100 indigenous tribes in the Amazon basin, and it appears that almost all groups in that area have a relationship with her, with only a couple of documented exceptions of which I'm aware.[12]

Here are a few of the dozens of names for Ayahuasca from the Amazon basin:

Caapi (meaning "leaf to make one exhale/become a spirit"), carpi, gahpi, yaje, cofa, oofa, kadana, kahi ide, sipo, mado bidada, rami-wetsem, natem.

Legend has it that Abuelita revealed the secrets of the brew to ancient peoples, during a time when humanity had taken a dark turn away from harmony, so that those people and their way of life may be preserved. And in some cases, those people live similarly now to how they have existed for thousands of years: deep in the jungle, with all of their needs met, in peace (the odd tribal skirmish notwithstanding) and contentedness.

In Amazonian culture, higher rates of exposure to Western influence is correlated with a less vibrant existence, but many have preserved their way of life. There are tribes deep in the Amazon which are extremely reclusive and refuse to make contact with outsiders.

For a case study of a culture that ritually works with Ayahuasca and have preserved their peaceful lifestyle, see the book, *The Continuum Concept.* No mention of Ayahuasca is made in the book, which focuses primarily on child care and social structure, but it is known that the Ye'kuana people who are the subject of the book do work with Ayahuasca. In the time since the book was published they have lost much of their traditional wisdom, which highlights the need to support these cultures in preserving their heritage in whatever way we can.

The main challenge I have experienced in working with

tribes with an unbroken hereditary lineage is the tendency for the tradition to become fixed and therefore fragile. In my view, the Huichol are a good example of a tribe that has swayed like a willow, rather than cracking in the middle like an ancient and brittle oak.

My ancestors, the Táltos, had an unbroken tradition for over 10,000 years, spanning back to the shamanic traditions of Siberia from where they originated (The word shaman is itself an Evenki or Tungus word from modern day Siberia and Mongolia).

When the Christians arrived in central Europe, the fixed nature of the hereditary traditions bent or broke to the onslaught against them. As many other traditions have over the last two millennia, they began practices such as storing their effigies under statues of saints. While they prayed in front of the saint, they were in fact praying to their Old Gods. Tragically, most of the old songs and rituals have been lost in time, and I never learned them in my childhood.

The unbroken traditions that remain today are aware of the effects that outside influence can have on their culture, and so most are understandably rigid and isolationist. Even within their own culture, the general approach is to keep it as fixed as possible, to preserve the traditions which they've inherited and to pass on that tradition to their descendants in as pure a form as possible.

While I respect and admire those who have kept their living traditions alive, I've seen that their culture is unsurprisingly most relevant to *their culture*. It is self referential, a feedback loop which outsiders, even if they have the privilege to be welcomed into a ceremony, are not likely to penetrate into in a meaningful and personally relatable way. Sadly, even the younger generations are mostly walking away from the old ways in hopes of finding greener grass, only to end up selling mobile phones or working in a sweatshop, or worse.

Put more simply, if you're in a Shipibo or Shuar ceremony you may receive profound healing but unless you plan to spend a decade with them it will not make you one of them. What it will do is *plant a seed* in you. Shamanic practice reminds you of what is fundamental about human existence, about your place in the web of life, and that knowledge is a seed which if tended and cared for will grow into your own connection with spirit. It will blossom into your pathway, helping you to hear the whispers of your ancestors and the wisdom of the plants.

The takeaway here is that shamanic practice is something alive, something which can be cultivated within yourself with tenderness and awareness. We must respect and protect the traditionalists keeping the old ways alive, while cultivating our own garden of inner guidance.

Today shamanism is seen as something "they" do by those who are uninitiated, rather than a personal connection with divine wisdom which is available to everyone. It is seen as going to a healer, rather than awakening and enlivening the inner healer and inner shaman.

We risk creating dogmas and rigid rules from the cultures and traditions of others, rather than exploring our own hearts. I believe everyone benefits from avoiding appropriation; we grow when we choose a fork in the road instead, guided by Spirit and the ancestors toward our own authentic path through the inner door.

Revivalist Shamanic Traditions

Revivalist traditions are ones which have been crushed under the wheel of time and oppression, and are now being brought back to life.

The image that comes to mind is that of a chain which has been broken, and the broken links spirited away and kept safe for the future. Today we are witnessing that future, the time of meeting ourselves again and reforging the broken links.
The greatest strength in revival is coming into direct contact with our ancestors and with the traditions of our blood, rather than seeking to appropriate practices from other traditions.

Táltos is one such tradition, and is going through revival in modern Hungary. Those broken links are being reforged, though no one can say with certainty if the links are in the original order, or if some links have been permanently misplaced and lost forever to time.

What's important here isn't that it's the *same*, but that it's relevant, that it *resonates* in the here and now.

I was once in ceremony with a hereditary Coast Salish medicine woman and her outlook on it was this:

"Each of you have shamanic ancestors who are waiting for you to listen to their guidance. You don't need to pretend to be First Nations, though you are welcome to join in our ceremonies in a good way.

You have your own way, and what's been forgotten can be remembered through the Creator. Be creative, spend your time being with the Creator. Many First Nations who died in the genocide are now being born to white parents. Listen to your young people, they come from the Creator and they can teach you a good way."

The biggest challenge I've experienced in revivalist traditions is the potential for argument and infighting over exactly *what* the tradition is, might have been, or should be.

Vegetalismo

Vegetalismo grew up around the rubber plantations of Iquitos and Pucallpa in the Peruvian rainforest, where Mestizos learned how to work with Ayahuasca from indigenous tribes such as the Shipibo-Conibo.

Vegetalistas – more commonly called curanderos, or sometimes Ayahuasceros, though the names are not precisely interchangeable – work with and learn from the plants and offer healing to their community, and to tourists. There is no formal structure to the practice, and no central organization, so rites of initiation are passed from plant, to teacher, to student, and the community they serve gauges their quality as a healer.

Some vegetalistas identify as Catholic, so vegetalismo can be seen as a bridge between indigenous use and the syncretic churches. The degree to which each vegetalista practices as a Catholic or a shamanic healer, is a completely individual choice.

Within vegetalismo, there are many individuals who are highly trained healers. But, there are also those who heard of an opportunity and only came to take advantage of it. In the jungle towns of Peru, especially Iquitos, Pucallpa, and Puerto Maldonado, waves of untrained individuals are flowing in to offer ceremonies with Ayahuasca. As you might imagine, this doesn't always end well for those who participate in their ceremonies.

Finding a well known and well respected teacher is important, for the safety of the journeyer. And, remember that power can change a humble teacher into a corrupt one; just because a healer was respected 5 years ago does not guarantee they are safe to work with now. Look for up to date information if you're journeying into the jungle.

Syncretic Churches

União do Vegetal and Santo Daime operate as legally recognized churches, with membership around the globe. I group them here for simplicity, though they are separate organizations. They combine several Christian practices and views with indigenous Ayahuasca use, as well as with practices of vegetalismo, and even African animism.

Individually, they have fought court battles with governments around the world to have their churches seen as legitimate, and have won nearly universally. This is a powerful statement in terms of how governments around the world are changing, and becoming more accepting.[13]

Modern Research

In recent years, Ayahuasca and other plant teachers have gained more attention from the scientific community, and are being studied as medicine for PTSD, depression, anxiety, cancer, and addictions treatment.

While much of the research is ongoing, early findings are encouraging, and support the benefits suggested by its long history of use.

Because of the rapidly expanding and evolving nature of the field, I suggest that you go to the source and visit the Multidisciplinary Association for Psychedelic Studies (MAPS) at http://maps.org for up to date research.

New Age Shamanism

What exactly is New Age shamanism? A precise answer is hard to pin down. With the exception of pristine indigenous traditions, which are on the verge of extinction, all shamanic traditions that exist today have some level of syncretism. Where do we draw the line between syncretic, Neo, and New Age shamanism?

I was once teaching at an international shamanic conference, and went to a journey guided by an elder of the community. She was a bright and light woman, advanced in her years and in her practice. During the journey, she was suddenly guiding us through layers of rainbow veils and talking about faeries and angels and Pleiadians... and I realized that her practice had quite a strong New Age flavour.

New Age shamans tend to work with crystals, but working with stones and crystals is as ancient as shamanism. New Age shamans tend to sing chants from all over the world, but so do syncretic shamans, and now even some Shipibo people are picking up chants from India and elsewhere. Should someone try and stop them?

What am I getting at here?

All of these divisions are *old paradigm thinking.*

Some say Jesus wanted the boundaries of the human heart to be dissolved, so that all the people of the world could look upon each other with love and kindness, the kind of love felt by the Creator.

And in a macabre and backwards way, the religion which bears his name has accomplished it with a globe sweeping genocide, and the scattering of so many traditions like spores on the wind.

Tribes from all around the world are coming together under one mottled flag. I know a Táltos who sings the Mahamrityunjaya Mantra along with traditional Hungarian folk songs while leading Ayahuasca ceremonies. The Huichol have a Christ and a Buddha in their pantheon along with grandfather Sun. There is a seminary in Goa where Christ is depicted with the Sun, Moon, and chakra system. And in Daime, Christian hymns are sung along with shamanic icaros.

Some have decried all this syncretism as New Age tomfoolery and the next step of colonialism, but none can deny that these are spiritually unprecedented times. Notice that all the mixing and borrowing isn't contained to privileged white Americans and Europeans; all over the world people are waking up and realizing that there is one universal love which flows through everything, and though it goes by many names the everflowing spring of kindness is all around us, all of the time.

The breaking of our shell has been painful, but now the light is shining through the cracks.

Regardless of the colour of our skin, we must act with **respect**. The Lakota, Dakota, and Nakota have declared war in tribal council against *Exploiters of Lakota Spirituality*. Indigenous people are working desperately to preserve their ways, to keep them sacred and to keep them for their descendants.

However one identifies, especially those from a Caucasian lineage, we must respect the teachings of our cousins and never teach what is not meant to be taught, or appropriate teachings that are not meant for outsiders.

One disturbing example which occurred was white Americans dancing the Ghost Dance without knowing its purpose. The Ghost Dance was for asking Spirit to cleanse America of white imperialists and return the First Nations to a clean way of living. By dancing the Ghost Dance, the whites were literally praying for their own extermination.

Whether we like it or not, the fabric of shamanism as it was has been torn and raped nearly to death. Shamans from around the world are taking those shattered pieces and creating a mosaic. We can idolize the past; ask indigenous people to not wear t-shirts or use plastic lawn chairs or drink

Pepsi so that white professors can study them in their "natural habitat".

The fact is that we shamans of every lineage are doing the best we can to weave a new tapestry, a new way of living that reclaims a harmonious and sustainable existence. They can scream cultural appropriation in the academic circles until they're blue in the face. While most academics are polishing the brass on the Titanic we're attempting to save our species from itself. If someone of Anglo-Saxon decent wants to go into the mountains with quartz crystals and pray to the faeries to find a deeper understanding of themselves, I believe we should support and encourage that as long as they respect the traditions and boundaries of other cultures.

Traditional vs. Modern Shamanism

Until approximately 30,000 years ago, most of humanity operated exclusively from the elemental consciousness of Earth (discussed in Part II). At that time, shamanism/animism was the *universal human religion.*

The wise souls were the shamans, healers, and tribal priests. They kept the simple, beautiful existence moving in its continuum.

Is that what you were taught in school? Why not?

The widely accepted modern view of our ancestors was put forward by philosophers such as Thomas Hobbes, who believed that prehistoric human life was, "*...continual fear, and danger of violent death... solitary, poor, nasty, brutish, and short.*" This idea has been a comfort to those of us living a modern life – living in concrete cubicles made by the dead for the living – assuring us that ours is a universally preferable existence.

In a world that was full of food, and barely populated at all – some estimates of population are as low as a couple thousand humans – they lived out their lives hunting, gathering, and making love. They only needed the help of the shamans and healers to keep them within their continuum of harmony, continuing to keep their root firmly planted. They lived simply, and expanded in population and territory *very* slowly.[14]

While this may sound like an Edenlike fantasy, modern archaeology and anthropology have confirmed that previous bleak outlooks on our past were wildly inaccurate and overstated, ice-age periods aside.[15]

The shamans developed and uncovered some valuable sacred tools, and formed strong relationships with helpful totemic plant and animal spirits, though rarely any higher spirits, as there was no need.

In many shamanic traditions, with exceptions such as the Q'eros, Tyronas, and a few others, the old traditions held that we should not directly connect with any "high level" spirits, which are sometimes grouped together simply as "Great Spirit" by one name or another, and instead connect only with intermediary spirits, and allow them to negotiate for us. These are the spirits that traditional shamanism works with; the ancestors, the elemental kingdom, earth-bound spirits, and totemic spirits working for our benefit.

Our needs were simply to have our state of harmony maintained while our species stabilized, and archaeology has shown that we faced near extinction several times during that process. In the hunter-gatherer lifestyle, a large, concentrated population is a problem, while a small mobile group means there's lots to go around.

Beginning some 30,000 years ago, and coming to a head 10,000 years ago, the average human consciousness began to radically transform. The pressure of spiritual evolution began to change the potency and maturity of the souls coming to Earth, with socially homogeneous baby souls, and fiery young souls becoming more common. This transition changed the consciousness of our species.

Today, we're experiencing a rapid spiritual, biological, and technological evolution, transitioning into a world where mature souls and the Air element are coming to prominence. However, there is a large gap to be made up: about 80% of humanity remains stuck in the level of consciousness associated with the element of Water, largely because of the dominant, suppressive nature of the element of Fire when out of balance.

Those who are firmly planted in Fire have ruled this world, and used their burning passion to suppress those they rule over. In their paradigm, the saying goes, "Whoever has the guns, has the power." Those who possess the Fire start the wars, and those who are in the element of Water are the ones doing the actual fighting.

This is making the transition of the times even more difficult for many, as they must transition through a phase of owning their power, their wilfulness and dynamism, before they can truly own the part of them that is ready to taste higher experiences.

It's like needing to learn to walk on land one day, and then experiencing flight the next; the gap is just too wide for most people without considerable support.

Ancient cultures called the paradigm we're transitioning out of the World of Fire, and no surprise, it's burning. During this transition, with its challenges, an opportunity has opened up for humanity: to reconnect with the Divine, no longer as a fetus attached to an umbilical cord, no longer perched on the edge of the nest where we were hatched, but soaring through the air on our own wings.

While the herd has abandoned spirituality out of necessity as predicted by ancient prophecies, those of us that have been preparing for this time over many lifetimes are poised to reap what we have sown; a higher level of human potential, centred in the element of Air.

To get there we will need as many tools as we can access – all of the spiritual paths developed over millennia – to unlock our hearts.

The world today holds a treasure trove of authentic spiritual paths ready to be walked, and many more which are simply fantasy and delusion.

Not surprisingly, the oldest tools, the oldest paths we know, the ones thoroughly tested and explored, are the ones which are the most precious. The well worn paths are the easiest to walk. Older is not strictly better, but the tried and true routes are often the most trustworthy as long as we know where we want them to take us.

Modern shamanism in general has the ultimate intention of clearing the path for our species to transition to the World of Air and beyond. This is accomplished through re-harmonizing us, re-attuning us to our continuum, and to our planet. This is necessary because Fire consciousness is a disharmonious state of consciousness, while Air consciousness is harmonious.

We need to overcome the polarization that exists within ourselves, reintegrate the dualities, to prepare ourselves for the challenges and opportunities of the times.

By World of Air, I essentially mean the Era of Air, the time when the dominant culture embraces the qualities associated with that element. No, I do not believe we will be receiving a new physical planet any time soon.

What does this rite of passage require? What are the obstacles we face? What does a recipe for our success look like? These are questions which hundreds, perhaps thousands of books have attempted to elucidate, and it boils down to some common themes.

The following stages don't happen in a linear fashion, rather they unfold in an "upward spiral" where you embody them more and more as you gain practice and understanding. This list is far from exhaustive, but may serve to outline your thinking.

- Detach and disentangle yourself from the illusion of this world, either by moving away from it, or, preferably, by moving through and transcending it. Move to a new level and let the old one die of neglect.

- Deal with your shit, your trauma, your history. Face your demons with kindness. Stop running and stop numbing out; the battle is at your doorstep.

- Reconnect with your essence, the part of yourself you covered up in order to survive as a child because it was not approved of, validated, or loved by your caregivers. Listen to your essence and the ancestors.

- See reality in all moments. In other words, awaken and transcend the limitations of subject and object. Seek the underlying truth of everything you encounter. Ask better questions, deeper questions.

- Accept what is and what has been; universally, without judgment, and without applying meaning. Do not resist or deny the past, focus instead on experiencing the present with as much clarity as possible. When the past surfaces as released emotions and memories, sit with them and let them pass. Just hear them.

- Discern your path. Become aware of the myriad choices which confront you in every moment, and consciously choose each step, aiming for the direction which calls you closer to your highest aspirations.

- Live with abandon. Live each minute as if you have 60 seconds to live and the clock is ticking. Waste no time, and yet, do not hurry.

- Forgive your enemies, forgive the ignorant and hurtful, forgive your parents, forgive yourself, forgive your life. There are no enemies, there are no villains. They are God wearing a villain mask, playing their part in the cosmic dance. If you ever hear yourself say "I cannot forgive *that*" consider the story of Palden Gyatso, a Tibetan monk who was imprisoned and tortured for 33 years and has forgiven his torturers. Forgiveness does not exclude accountability. We often resist forgiveness because we think it means that we are OK with whatever trauma happened, and this is not true. We can accept what happened, forgive those involved, and take steps so that it does not happen again.

- Walk forward in kindness, patience, understanding, and with purpose. We aren't aiming for perfection; there is no "there." Focusing on getting to a final destination, a state of perfection, is inevitably counter productive. Instead, asking, "*Am I living my purpose in this life in this moment? If not, what can I do right now to be more in alignment with my essence? If I cannot hear my essence, what can I do right now to move toward removing the blockages between myself and my Self? How can I get out of my own way?*" Again, asking deeper questions.

Part II of this book goes into greater depth on how you can take shamanic wisdom from ceremonies out into your daily life. This may seem a separate issue from modern shamanism, but we must remember the oldest and perhaps most accurate translation of the word shaman:

"*She who sees in the dark.*"

It is a task shared by all to become the light that sees in the darkness, to illuminate our own paths, and then to be a light for others. Not by force or by propounding doctrine, but through becoming a humble, living example, from the inside out. By walking a path of spiritual evolution, and offering to others, "*I'm walking in this direction. You're welcome to walk with me, if you choose.*"

Traditional shamanism was simple because simple was all that was required. When you are metaphorically crawling on your belly, your choices are limited.

As we learn to soar, our choices become infinitely more complex. The tools we must use if we intend to live in harmony become more dynamic and complex. This is the gift of our times: a treasure chest of dynamic tools, to be used as needed. It's also the curse of our times: an infinite array of bewildering choices.

The way out is through, and following your inner guidance will get you on a good path.

Witchcraft and Shamanism

Dark witchcraft (called brujeria negra in Spanish) and shamanism represent polar opposites of the same spectrum.

In both, the universe is seen as an infinite and unfathomable creation, embodied and animated by subtle forces. The difference lies in how each relates to those forces: dark witchcraft attempts to use power to bend those forces to human will, while shamanism harmonizes with positive and beneficial power, for healing and to align humanity with the universe.

Shamanic people build a village next to the river, rather than redirecting the river to the village.

In your own assessment of a shaman and whether or not you're safe with them, a fundamental question is, "*Do they seek to bend themselves to spirit, or bend spirit to them?*"

Plastic Shamans

What is a plastic shaman?

A close friend from Lima once confided in me that the majority of people from Lima have a poor opinion of Ayahuasca and Wachuma, of shamanic practice, and of both the Andean and Amazonian people in general.

And yet, waves of people are moving from the Peruvian capital back to the Amazon. For some, their roots are in the Amazon and they had lived in Lima simply to survive and eke out a living.

For them Ayahuasca tourism has been a great blessing which has enabled them to return to their ancestral homes, and I've been told by some Amazonians that outside interest in Amazonian shamanism has helped counter the myth of the "American dream" which is so damaging to traditional cultures.

Most people from Lima and elsewhere know nothing of shamanism, nothing of healing, but they smell money in the jungle just as their ancestors did when they encountered the rubber tree.

Land in the Amazon is almost free, Ayahuasca grows wild, labour is very cheap, and anyone can set up a website these days. As a result, starting a retreat centre and making it appear legitimate could hardly be easier.

The biggest threat is when these centres are started by brujas posing as shamans. This leads to the "Zombie kids of Iquitos", tourists who have come in search of healing or excitement and have been emotionally, mentally, and spiritually damaged by brujas (witches).

In my experience, there is no way that we can definitively say one way is "right" without discounting tribes or groups who are working with spiritual integrity and offering seekers true help. To me, as long as there is honesty, intention, and spiritual integrity, then a path or teacher is "right", though not every path is right for every seeker.

Integrity means that in addition to basic safety and keeping their word, the space holder *doesn't claim to be anything they are not.*
What this most often looks like is white Americans claiming to be native and holding native ceremonies. Or, holding New Age ceremonies and calling them traditional native ceremonies.

I think you get the picture; the issue is taking from a culture and saying *"I'm one of them!"* Of course, you can be taught and initiated by an elder in a specific tradition, and then teach or lead ceremony with the blessing of that elder and the tribe. This usually takes 10-16 years of living with the tribe if you are dedicated and sincere.

I have my own tradition which values the teachings of all plants and totemic spirits, from Amanita to Zacatechichi. You have your own tradition too somewhere in your blood, probably only a few generations back.

Part II:
Elemental Wisdom of the Ancestors

The intention of part II is to prepare you emotionally, psychologically, and spiritually for the intense inner work involved in participating in shamanic rituals, ceremonies, rites, and ordeals. Integration after a ceremony is at least as important as preparation, and so we'll go into depth about how to integrate after a ceremony and bring that wisdom into your life.

It's beneficial to have these understandings now, so that you will be able to spend as much time as possible immersed in a state of "learning by doing" during a ceremony, rather than needing to spend precious time on covering theory there. Depending on who you're sitting with, the information you get before a ceremony might be as brief as, "Sit down and drink this."

Why did I write this book? So that anyone coming to a ceremony I was leading would be primed with a deeper understanding of shamanic practice, which would allow us all to go much more deeply into the practice without spending too much time on theory.

The topics covered herein are profoundly deep, and literally tens of thousands of pages have been written on them. What I offer is an overview, a kind of spiritual "connect-the-dots" to get your process started, which you may explore in depth within yourself during a ceremony. I also offer you practices on preparing for the ceremony and integrating afterwards, which will help you to bring shamanism into your daily life.

I practice a blend of ancient spiritual traditions, though they're not randomly tossed together. While I inherited a hereditary shamanic tradition through my blood, I am fundamentally a syncretic practitioner, "one who mixes."

I inherited the tradition of Táltos in a shattered state, crushed by hundreds of years of oppression, and in my practice I fit in puzzle pieces from my cousins where there were gaps in my own understanding.

My grandmother died when I was in my teens, leading me to search out shamanic teachers from traditions which resonate with my blood and the ways of my ancestors. I've been blessed to have experienced the old ways of the Huichol, Celts, Siberians, Tibetans, North American First Nations, and the Peruvian Andeans and Amazonians. I share this with you as we transition into these deeper perspectives, so you have some idea of the path I've walked. I don't claim to be a teacher in these traditions, only eternally grateful for the teachings and kindness of my cousins.

To some, the information I'm about to share will naturally make sense and be recognized as being self-evident. For others, it may seem abstract, paradoxical, and unnecessarily mystical.

All I ask is that you approach these topics with maturity. Maturity meaning that as a child you were encoded with beliefs, which became held as truths, and some have gone unexamined. I ask you to evaluate these teachings based on who you are and where you're at **now**, the world you live in now, in contrast to the one you were raised in. I ask that you take personal responsibility for your perspectives.

Don't give up responsibility to your culture, your parents, your generation, your religion of origin, or any other force outside of yourself.

One of the greatest challenges in sharing this work is that we all have preconceived notions of how things should be, based not on our present needs but on our conditioning. This is especially difficult because most people will unconsciously reference their past experiences with ascetic religions, which includes nearly all mainstream religions.

An ascetic religion or spiritual practice is one which aims to achieve spiritual growth through distancing one's self from everyday mundane reality, through prayer and broadly applied abstinence. The mundane world is viewed as a distraction, a nearly hellish illusion, which is to be ignored and denied whenever possible.

The alternative, is to "dive into" reality, go into sensations and experiences, and fully live them to achieve spiritual growth. As in modern science, we aim to experience and examine the world, rather than believe we already know everything. This approach of "diving in" doesn't have a name I find sufficiently succinct, but it's shared by the Taoists, Tantrics, shamans, and druids among others. The most broad name might be the "Mystery Traditions." It has been proposed that all of the Mystery Traditions of the East and West fundamentally stem from ancient shamanic mysticism.

The attitudes of the Mystery Traditions are intensely challenging for practitioners of asceticism for several reasons. Asceticism requires extreme long term commitment, a commendable "long term pain, long term gain" approach, which we know from history few humans are actually capable of accomplishing.

For example: to an ascetic practitioner – be they Catholic or Vedantic – who has abstained from absolutely all sexual activity for 30 years, the sacred sexual practices of Taoism, Tibetan Buddhism, shamanism, or Tantra are extremely threatening because they are not only techniques proven through time to be effective paths of spiritual growth, they are demonstrably faster than the ascetic approach. In a comparatively short span of dedicated practice, they offer immediate benefits on all levels, rather than promising, "*You'll get yours in the next life/afterlife.*"

Asceticism is a simple though difficult approach, requiring little technique, while the Mystery approach is highly technical. There are countless ways of practising without any strictly right or wrong ways. What matters in a Mystery teaching is the outcome, the measurable internal effects. It's important that you understand that *I do not think that there is any one "right" way.*

I do know from my own experience, and from the experiences of the hundreds of individuals I have worked with personally, that the way we do things **works** for many people. They become healthier on all levels, they experience spiritual connection that few alive today can possibly comprehend, and a host of other benefits which are immediately experienced, readily tangible, and profoundly rewarding.

At the same time, there is an ever present risk of taking a turn which does not work, which requires one to be constantly aware, constantly evaluating effects, and to be on guard for hubris.

I am not at all interested in attempting to find a "right way", and I do not care about how anyone else is practising their spirituality, or how they may perceive our practices. I am singlemindedly focused on practising in a way that *works*.

Therefore, I ask that you approach with a discerning "don't know mind" and just try things on. See if they fit for you, in the same way that you would try on a pair of jeans before purchasing them. I'm not asking you to "buy what I'm selling", just encouraging you to try it on. See if it suits you, both in theory and more importantly in **practice**, and then decide for yourself.

I fully encourage skepticism, meaning the practice of critically assessing what's being offered with a discerning mind and heart. But a fatalistic attitude, meaning, "Nothing works for me. This won't work for me because I'm [*insert limiting belief*]" will not serve you.

Ceremonial time, practice time, is best spent immersing yourself in the "Being" rather than theory. Focusing on the practical steps of achieving better health, a cleaner self on all levels, becoming a spiritual Warrior of Light, connecting with Divine Love and forgiveness, finding your place in the universe, strengthening concentration of the mind, having direct spiritual experience, spending time with the Creator, and so on.

If on reading this last paragraph you noticed yourself feeling cynical, I don't blame you. A caterpillar cannot imagine the freedom of being a butterfly, and unless you've had experiences of boundless freedom, I don't expect you to take my renditions at face value.

Remember: 1 minute of practice is often worth an entire day of learning theory.

"Who Am I?"

Looking at the human being, we are composed of many elements, many facets, and there are infinite lenses through which we can view ourselves and our structures.

At our core we're composed of nothingness or emptiness, which is then impregnated and animated by layers of spirit. Our physical bodies and all of the material creation which we perceive through our five senses, the manifest world, are constructed by a type of spirit called the elementals.

The elemental spirits govern the energies that we are primarily composed of, Earth, Water, Fire, and Air.

The transcendental elements are Space and Consciousness, the sandbox and thought pattern blueprint for all creation. Beyond the thought pattern is the Creator, the source of everything which encompasses all.

When applied personally, each of these elements can be interchangeably thought of as attributes, sensations, or states of the physical, emotional, mental, or spiritual self.

For example, you can have an Earthy body, physical state, feeling, or thought. The quality of being "Earthy", or of any other element, can be expressed in any area of your experience of life. You may have an Airy body, Fiery energy, Watery emotions, and an Earthy mind, or any such combination. However, most people are dominated by one or two elemental influences.

The elemental world-view was nearly universal throughout

spiritually advanced ancient cultures with variations on the theme, and is central to a broad spectrum of healing practices stretching all the way from before the Egyptians to the modern Jungians.

Many teachings refer to fractal polarity (duality at all levels except the source), the three worlds, and between four to ten elements. They aim to transform the two passive, receptive elements, Earth and Water, using the two dynamic elements, Fire and Air, into the higher elements, Space, Consciousness, and union with Source.

The ancient traditions I've encountered vary in practice, themes, and details, though their destination and intention is universal. Some say there are more, or fewer elements, and they relate the elements to human experience in a variety of ways. Keep this in mind as you follow along: what I express here is just one perspective, a perspective which I've found to be valuable for myself and many others.

One answer to the question, "Who Am I?" is "*I am a holographic representation of all that is above, and all that is below. I am a microcosm of the macrocosm.*"
This is the alchemical *Law of Correspondence*, and is an important facet of the discussion around elements.

Elements exist within you, and those same elements are present in every galaxy, and every subatomic particle: they are present throughout the entire manifest universe. Through working with them within yourself, you align yourself with the harmony of creation.

What does that mean practically? How do we apply that concept, and take it from just an esoteric thought, into something that we can extract practical value from?

While reading the following sections, you may understandably conclude that I'm speaking about something symbolic, not literal, not something which can be grasped. Again, some practice and patience will help it all to make sense; you'll get it when you feel it.

For concepts to be transformed into something more concrete, first we have to understand what we're working with, in the same way that a potter's fingers understand clay, a baker knows flour, and an herbalist speaks with the plants. Once we have a basic understanding of our material, then we can start manipulating it, and experientially evaluate the effects firsthand.

Direct experience is necessary since our material is something ephemeral which cannot be grasped in the hands, though it can be experienced subjectively through the five senses with practice, and also by observing moods and emotions moving through you which relate to a corresponding element.

The descriptions of the elements that follows come primarily from shamanic views.
An effort has been made to avoid adulterated modern interpretations, with the exception of associating certain states of mind with each element. This line of thinking was conceptualized by Carl Jung, and isn't a part of any ancient tradition that I'm familiar with.

However, I believe that focusing on the movement of emotion

92

has become vitally important in this era of Fire dominating Water. The ebb and flow of emotions and the psychic energy which they indicate paint a picture of how we can better relate to our inner experiences.

As you read about the different elements, ask yourself, *"Which qualities are most natural and dominant in me? Which qualities could I benefit from cultivating inside myself?"*

The Element of Earth

First you must have a container to work within, a crucible. Without a strong, pure crucible, you don't have a foundation for transformation, and this foundation is symbolized by Earth; vitality, physical health, and a grounded pragmatic approach.

When considering building a foundation for spiritual growth and evolution, from the shamanic perspective, you must walk toward solid health. Otherwise you're building a temple on a foundation of sand.

While the element of Earth is less complicated than the others, and therefore has fewer issues, it can be lacking in strength. When weak, you work to build it up, in the same way you would build up, thicken, and harden the walls of a clay pot.
When Earth is lacking, you drag yourself through your days.

When too strong or out of balance, this can induce a state of being "thickheaded" or close minded, and being "earthbound", or too focused on the mundane to be open to experiencing spiritual connection. The best approach in that case is generally to work on increasing the other elements within yourself, especially Fire which will help to pull the energy upward.

When considering the historical role of shamanic practice, it most often related to the Earth element: curing the sick, negotiating with animal spirits for a good hunt, working with totemic spirits for protection from predators and dark spirits, guidance toward a safe place to set up a village, and so on.

94

Today, we're more interested in the transcendent spiritual wisdom of shamanism than with the physical day-to-day practicalities; we're more concerned with purging emotional parasites than physical ones.

However, while life has changed radically and humanity has mostly transitioned to the consciousness of Water or Fire, the element of Earth may be more important than ever.

Earth is the element which allows the inner human to interface with manifest existence, and without it there is no humanity. In other words, if you're not grounded, if you don't have a foundation of *physical life*, how can you hope to accomplish anything? This may sound like an absurd thought, yet it's one that the ancient peoples are screaming into the modern ear:
"If you kill the Earth, where will you live?"

And so, we must collectively come back to ourselves, and come back to basics if we hope to survive the present era.

After each element, I'll describe practices for increasing that element inside of yourself. When doing these activities, you will have a stronger effect if you do them with *intention*.

Offer it as a prayer to the Creator and give it away, and then state why you're going to do what you're doing. "It's my intention to build stronger Earth energy in my body while I plant these seeds in the Earth, for increased health and vitality." Saying it with emotion, conviction, and purpose will make it that much stronger.

Practices for Strengthening Earth

- Walk barefoot on bare ground.

- Drum in a rhythmic monotonous beat while closing your eyes and going inside yourself; drum journey.

- Eat healthy food in generous quantities.

- Body scanning meditation; sit on the ground with your legs stretched out in front of you. Grasp your legs or feet with your hands wherever it's comfortable and relax your back. Close your eyes, and allow your inner focus to travel from your sitting bones, up your back, down your arms, to your feet, and back to your sitting bones in a circuit of awareness. Do this slowly with your mind while you relax, focus on your connection to the Earth, and breath deeply for 5-10 minutes or more. This practice is most beneficial if done every day.

- Take time to sit on the ground or even nap on the ground, preferably out in nature. Camping and hiking are similarly effective.

- Work out and build your strength with exercise. Get in touch with your physical body and give it love and support.

- Spend time in a home in the woods immersed in nature, or better yet, live in the woods.

- Start a garden, get dirt under your fingernails and watch plants grow. *As simple as this sounds, out of this whole book this one sentence might be the best advice I can give you.*

- For a more in-depth and powerful practice, see the Earth Ritual for Rooted Strength on page 160

Your intention relating to Earth is to achieve outstanding physical health and a state of vibrant vitality from which you can focus on higher intentions.

The Element of Water

Within your physical, energetic, emotional and mental systems, Water is the element most susceptible to going out of balance and being problematic.

The Water becomes impure, static, toxic, and even poisonous. Water relates to our sexuality and creativity, and just as it is the element which dominates the surface of the Earth, it's also the element which most strongly influences humankind. Shamanic work focuses on cleansing and purifying your Water, and also on increasing and strengthening the other elements within you.

There is nothing at all "wrong" with the element of Water of course, it's fundamental to life. In the same vein, just because we've polluted the ocean with crude oil, nuclear waste, billions of tonnes of plastic, and other toxins, so much so that it's on the verge of total ecosystem collapse, that doesn't mean there's anything wrong with the *ocean*; it's not the oceans fault.

Here we see the *Law of Correspondence* in action. We pollute ourselves, and we pollute the world around us. When we clean ourselves, we clean the world around us.

We have a great overabundance of Water, and most of us are lacking in Earth, Fire, and Air. This pollution and imbalance leads to a "toxic-swamp" like condition, resulting in depression, lethargy, sexual dysfunction, addiction, jealousy, attachment, confusion, living in a fantasy world (rose coloured glasses), distraction, fatalistic attitude toward life, indecisiveness, and heavy duty neurosis.

I believe that most of the population of the developed world is struggling with too much toxic Water on all levels, resulting in a disharmonious and out of balance world-view where self annihilating behaviours are normalized through excessive fantasizing and cultural indoctrination.

The pollution is self-replicating, because if you're pumped full of toxic Water you can delude yourself into thinking that a magic bullet solution will be found by *someone, somehow*, while walking down the tragic path of consume and destroy.

As such, the purification, distillation, and transformation of the Water element within us is one of the primary areas of focus for our efforts. This allows the Water to return to its true nature; a beautiful life force, the creative wellspring which inspires everything,

It can be tempting to give up, to "dump" the Water. However, this is an attitude we must collectively overcome if the human species is to survive, since there is no difference between "in here" and "out there". Taking personal responsibility is a major challenge of our times.

A huge amount of energy is stored in Water, and so you must instead clean, move, and transform it within yourself, and never attempt to solve a problem by dumping it on someone else. Leading up to a shamanic ceremony, it's normal to undertake Dieta to cleanse and prepare your body. This furthers your intention of cleansing and balancing of the Water element within you.

The Dieta is like a piece of cloth with activated charcoal in it, providing a loose yet effective filtration of the Water energy within you. Once you arrive at a ceremony your work shifts to more precise, subtle purification of the Water, to circulation and transformation.

The more thorough purification of Water during ceremony is like transforming groundwater into distilled water: on casual observation, you might not be able to tell the difference, but their properties and effects are substantially different.

Distilled water is completely pure down to the subtlest level (*deepened*), no longer conducts electricity (*discharged*), is more acidic than typical water (*penetrating*), and is a stronger solvent than spring water (*dissolving*). Yet if you compare the two casually they appear the same. The ceremonial work is like this; you walk out of the ceremony still human, but a *changed* human. Perhaps even *more* human.

This is one of many reasons why Dieta is valuable. Without it, you would spend much of your time performing the basic cleansing in the sacred space rather than dedicating that precious time toward larger aspirations. By preparing yourself before a ceremony and taking time to integrate afterwards you make the process more profound and more gentle on your whole system.

Keeping the Water within you pure is challenging, because every aspect of modern culture heavily pollutes it; processed foods, Hollywood romances, the news, advertising, ingrained comparison and judgment, pharmaceuticals, environmental toxins, conformity and indoctrination, and essentially everything which subtly communicates "**You suck! You're not enough!**"

Practices for Purifying Water

- Take a long relaxing Epsom salt bath with essential oils. Magnesium deficiency is common in most modern populations, while extreme stress and a chaotic mind are nearly universal. This is an inexpensive, effective, and pleasant experience which is beneficial to your whole system. Indigenous peoples from around the world value bathing in hot springs and consider them sacred and this is a similar practice.

- Turn off the news, turn off the gossip, turn off social media, turn off your smart phone. Water is the element of gregariousness and can easily spill overboard. Think of what happens when a droplet of water hits a lake; it dissolves. Take time to stop thinking about what other people are doing, feeling, saying, and thinking. This will force you to spend more time with yourself; your own inner sensations.

- Watch your addictive patterns and cravings, and become conscious of them, realizing that you always have a choice in every moment. We go into greater depth about this in the chapter on Consciousness on page 130.

- Practice being more discerning, and less judgmental. The choices of other people have nothing to do with you. Let them be. If someone makes a choice which impacts you in a negative way, regardless of who that person is to you, recognize that you always have a choice. You always have the ability to make a statement of discernment, "That behaviour isn't what I choose for my life. You're welcome to do what works for you, and I am now removing myself from this situation because it doesn't work for me." This statement eliminates judgment while empowering you to make healthier choices for yourself.

- Perform a ritual on the beach where you express gratitude for the life giving quality of the oceans and of Water. Make an offering to the spirits of Water, and then silently observe the sea for some time while contemplating its virtuous qualities. As Lao Tzu said, *"True goodness is like water, it benefits everything and harms nothing. It ever seeks the lowest place, the place that all others avoid."*
  Take some time to notice how this soft element eventually breaks down and penetrates all resistance in time.

- Draw, paint, write, dance, or sculpt. Engage your artistic creative energies in producing *something*. Don't worry about creating a masterpiece, the point is to get the *juices flowing*. When you're feeling the tide of shadow aspects of Water rising, especially around the full moon, remember that the negative emotions and sensations are aspects of yourself which are begging to be heard, past hurts needing an outlet. Let them out, then turn to practices which can bring you to a higher state of consciousness.

- Get involved with spiritual practices which stir, elevate, and warm the cold, wet, heavy nature of Water. Often the best thing you can do for Water is to stop pouring the toxic thoughts and behaviours into the cistern and get active!

- See the Water Ritual for Forgiveness and Release on page 165.

Your intention for the Water energy within your system is to cleanse it and circulate it on the physical, energetic, emotional and mental levels.

The Element of Fire

You have your Earthen container, you have Water in it, next you require a catalyst, that magic ingredient which makes everything move.

The urge to inspire, the dynamic, energized, and enthusiastic energy. Fire is associated with strong digestion and immune system, strong leadership, charisma, and when out of balance, explosive violence and dominance.

Stoke this energy, and learn to follow its natural upward direction. The upward motion becomes a significant focus; this is when the work really starts to transform, when you start moving beyond simple intentions and toward higher aspirations. You become a rocket ship filling with fuel, preparing to depart from the mundane, the *mundus*, the everyday world. The element of Fire is what powers a more refined purification, and generates upward motion of energy.

The heat of Fire radiating like the Sun is what turns the Water into steam, leaving the impurities behind to be transmuted, composted, or burned. The "steam" now becomes your vehicle for spiritual evolution and directs your path.

Embodied with heat, the energy of Water is transformed as it rises and is put to work. Symbolically, you can imagine a clay pot with Water inside surrounded by Fire, generating steam. The steam is rising to spin a turbine and the spinning of the turbine generates electricity.

The rising energy transitions to higher states, and generates a much more subtle, mysterious, and powerful energy.

This imagery accurately represents shamanic practice: you get grounded, you elevate the parts of yourself which are stuck in darkness. You use willpower, courage, and the warrior spirit to create a change, and you direct this rising energy, this rising force, toward the heart. And from there, toward higher aspirations.

Fire is the elemental energy that supports you in pushing yourself toward your intentions, lights a fire under your butt. It makes you feel, "I'm worth it! I'm going to do it!" Without Fire, everything has a lacklustre quality to it.

Discipline, discernment, and delaying gratification are powered by Fire, fuelling you toward the things in life which you are passionate about, which your soul is crying out for. Without this quality, nothing in life goes far, whether it's working life, spiritual life, or any other endeavour worth pursuing.

This is where the burning desire to heal, grow, release, and connect is forged. It is the element most strongly associated with masculinity, patriarchy, and warrior culture.

When moved up, melded with love, compassion, and kindness, it is the "burning heart" that defends the weak and disempowered. A loving protective parent that would fight to the death to save their beloved child. Western motivational programs often aim to spark this kind of Fire in people.

While you're building the Fire, know that many impurities will be burned up, meaning you'll need to face the shadow as well as the light as the pendulum swings inside of you – hopefully finding a healthy balancing point in the end.

You may find yourself reacting disproportionately and boiling with rage in situations where you would have sulked in the past. You might overstep boundaries without even realizing it and need to temper yourself as you discover new levels of self confidence. In the end, be kind to yourself, you're learning to advocate for yourself.

If you find yourself simmering and the anger frightens you, remind yourself that this is an impurity being burned off. **Do not allow yourself to become an abuser!** You are fully responsible for your reactions. Find a healthy environment to process the impurities, such as the following practices.

Practices for Building Inner Fire

- Almost every form of martial arts is highly effective at increasing willpower and internal Fire. Some are specifically non-violent in their aim, such as Aikido and Shorinji Kempo.

- Stare into a camp fire or candle without blinking, and focus your attention unwaveringly on one point. While doing this, feel the warmth of the element coming into the core of your body. Do this for 10 minutes or more.

- A traditional fire-walking ceremony is an ancient method of working with the flames, though it's critical that the ceremony be lead by someone qualified.

- Sweat lodge, temazcal, or other forms of dry sauna can strongly increase the Fire. When combined with ritual and ceremony, the effect is multiplied many times. If you're participating in a sweat lodge choose your

- See the Fire Ritual for Increasing Auspices of the Sun on page 172.

Your intention for the Fire energy within your system is to build, balance, contain, and direct it.

The Element of Air

Air represents the transition point between matter and spirit, the in between place that's there and yet not quite there. Matter, yet insubstantial. You cannot see the air move, but you can see the rustling of the leaves.

The energy of Air is associated with unconditional love, selflessness, detachment and non-possessiveness – as opposed to the jealous and attached love related with Water. In this state, there's no need to ask, "What's in it for me?" because it is evident beyond question that all you could need is present.

A classic example of this element is the love of a parent for an infant. Neither ever ask, *"Does this child deserve the best? Is this child worthy of milk, warmth, and tenderness?"* both the child and the parent know the answer to these questions is an emphatic **yes** in the core of their being, and history has shown that attempting to change this attitude of fundamental compassion and deserving leads to disastrous results on a societal scale.

This giving nature lives in each of us, because we are all receivers; we have all been blessed to drink from the well of life.

Consider this:

"You give but little when you give of your possessions. It is when you give of yourself that you truly give.

For what are your possessions but things you keep and guard for fear you may need them tomorrow?

And tomorrow, what shall tomorrow bring to the overprudent dog burying bones in the trackless sand as he follows the pilgrims to the holy city?

And what is fear of need but need itself?
Is not dread of thirst when your well is full, the thirst that is unquenchable?

There are those who give little of the much which they have--and they give it for recognition and their hidden desire makes their gifts unwholesome.

And there are those who have little and give it all.
These are the believers in life and the bounty of life, and their coffer is never empty.

There are those who give with joy, and that joy is their reward.
And there are those who give with pain, and that pain is their baptism.

And there are those who give and know not pain in giving, nor do they seek joy, nor give with mindfulness of virtue;
They give as in yonder valley the myrtle breathes its fragrance into space.
Through the hands of such as these God speaks, and from behind their eyes He smiles upon the earth.

It is well to give when asked, but it is better to give unasked, through understanding;
And to the open-handed the search for one who shall receive

is joy greater than giving.

And is there aught you would withhold?
All you have shall some day be given;
Therefore give now, that the season of giving may be yours
and not your inheritors'.

You often say, "I would give, but only to the deserving."
The trees in your orchard say not so, nor the flocks in your
pasture.

They give that they may live, for to withhold is to perish.
Surely he who is worthy to receive his days and his nights, is
worthy of all else from you.

And he who has deserved to drink from the ocean of life
deserves to fill his cup from your little stream.

And what desert greater shall there be, than that which lies
in the courage and the confidence, nay the charity, of
receiving?

And who are you that men should rend their bosom and
unveil their pride, that you may see their worth naked and
their pride unabashed?

See first that you yourself deserve to be a giver, and an
instrument of giving.

For in truth it is life that gives unto life while you, who deem
yourself a giver, are but a witness.

And you receivers... and you are all receivers... assume no

weight of gratitude, lest you lay a yoke upon yourself and upon him who gives.
Rather rise together with the giver on his gifts as on wings;

For to be overmindful of your debt, is to doubt his generosity who has the freehearted earth for mother, and God for father."

~Kahlil Gibran, On Giving

The question arises,
"*Why don't we treat everyone this way?*"

Looking in the mirror, what do you feel the person you see deserves? Should the person gazing back at you feel guilt for having received their days and their nights from the wellspring of life?

Take a moment now, and look in the mirror, repeatedly asking the person you meet there,

"***What do you deserve?***"

Go ahead and do that now...
I'll wait here; I won't look......

For most of the human population, the biggest challenge with Air is that it simply isn't activated, and this is obvious by observing human behaviour for even a few moments. Most people are so caught up in worldly affairs, they haven't considered their inner landscape.

Achieving a lighter state, an opening of the heart, is perhaps

111

the most important intention of our times. We kill animals because we have distanced ourselves from the profound suffering we put them through for our pleasure.

We have numbed our hearts to how consumer culture is rapidly depleting the materials of our planet. We have turned a blind eye to the genocide which has been inflicted upon the indigenous people of the world. And many more atrocities, too many to name here.

The dominant culture on the Earth today has collectively turned a blind eye to all this suffering and much more because of a belief that, *"I am me, and everything outside of my skin is not me. If it's not me or my family, I don't care."*

This perspective reveals shallow thinking and shallow feeling. If the ecosystems of the Earth die, how could any of us hope to survive? My point is not about environmentalism, it's that while humans are primarily concerned with *surviving, fitting in,* and *capitalizing,* we're ignoring the higher intentions of *universal love, harmony,* and *deep thought.*

These latter three are not luxuries; more than ever in our history, they are humanity's best hope for survival.

But, reaching these lofty intentions follows a winding road. I've heard it said, with the best intentions, "Focus on your heart... go to your heart... open your heart..." and it can't hurt since where attention goes, energy flows.

But, it can be like saying, "Focus on Spuzzum, go to Spuzzum..." and if one has never been to the small town of Spuzzum, it's meaningless; it's like telling a heavy smoker to follow their nose. Our sensitivity to the part of us that guides us to the heart has been damaged by the searing smoke of civilization.

To experience this higher energy, which dances with the transpersonal and transcendental, we must *practice* with focused intent. There are countless practices, from many traditions, which can assist us in elevating our energy to the realm of Air, to the place of universal love.

Subtly working with the subconscious is important because it is the subconscious which truly runs the show. So, we focus on healing the subconscious first, which is perhaps the only way to make this journey easier; to remove the deeply held obstacles and governors which keep us doing the same old behaviours. I will go into greater depth about this in the next section.

The lack of deserving which so many of us experience, the lack of self-forgiveness, self-compassion, self-trust, self-gentleness, self-respect, and self-adoration, are some of the greatest hurdles that we must overcome. As soon as you read "self-adoration", did you hear a tiny voice tell you, "That's for self-centred people, you're here to push yourself and work hard, to be busy and productive!"

While I applaud you if you've purged the undeservingness down to your deepest core, the truth is that after thousands of years of living in slavery or borderline slavery, or slavery that feels like freedom despite the fact that you're never free no matter how much of it you accumulate, most of our species is deeply ingrained in the surviving-conforming-winning mode of thinking.

Many of us have been caught in the illusion that, "Once I'm earning more money, I'll feel safer and more comfortable, then I'll start relaxing and untangling the knots inside myself." Only to realize that some unseen force prevents us from experiencing the peace and abundance that we think we are seeking.

And yet when we travel the world, we can find literally millions of examples of simple people, living simple lives, far below what we call the "poverty line" who want for nothing outside of the life they have, until an outside force tells them that what they have is not enough. Then the younger generation feel inadequate, and they leave to get an education and end up working in sweatshops.

The internal transition that leads us to the type of universal trust where we are happy and content regardless of external factors doesn't ever come from external pursuits; the rat race is a treadmill.

Deep and lasting peace comes from a deep experience of being at one with all. By that, I mean a knowing that you are fundamentally a part of nature, a pixel in the art of the universe.

Paradoxically, finding that peace often starts with an inner hunger, a deep knowing that something needs to change internally, and the urgent resolve of a drowning person. A call from within from the inner healer, drawing us back into the continuum of ourselves.

This is a paradoxical unity: complacency leads to a slow and boring death and a life left unlived, while desperation can lead eventually to an unbreakable peace. This is because of the difference between the two kinds of peace: peace from being comfortably numb, and peace from acceptance, trust, and self knowledge.

Seeking comfort is self-centred, while seeking peace from the inside out, through aligning yourself with the Macrocosm is perhaps the most beneficial activity which a human has the ability to undertake. When we see ourselves reflected in everything, and everything reflected in the people we love, only the sociopaths among us can continue to kill the world.

So, who can we blame?

We can blame the small group of individuals, less than 1% of humanity, that are actively trying to cause harm and keep the human heart closed with pain and pressure, and we can direct anger at them if we choose.

However, we then become the ones burdened by living in anger, while they continue to impoverish our planet and our species.

So, what is a solution?

Forgive yourself; you are just a single tiny human being, and berating and judging yourself for every imperfection only distracts you from living your purpose.

Focusing on inconsequential failings in yourself only serves to blind you from the light of your inner divinity. Conversely, *living from your divinity* aligns you with forces that serve to generate a harmonious relationship with the rest of humanity, with our planet and the other species who inhabit her, and with forces beyond.

Who has not heard the phrase, *"Be the change you want to see in the world"*?

Said another way, *"Embody the world you wish to create, create the world you wish to inhabit, and the old one dissolves out of neglect."*

Observe every action you take, every choice you follow through with. Ask yourself, *"If everyone made this choice, how would the world look?"*

But first you must overcome inertia, and a prison with transparent bars. Given how uncomfortable the work we undertake is in shamanic practice, you can congratulate yourself for how far you've come, glancing back at the tracks you are leaving on the path to deter perfectionism and despair, and encourage yourself to keep walking. Because, there is no "there."

When we blame, we shovel garbage from our yard into our neighbours. Instead, we can all achieve more by taking personal responsibility for our own choices. Every day, take a small step toward living in the kind of world you want for your great-grandchildren by taking personal responsibility for a problem and making a better choice, so that they will have an easier time.

Because many of us grew up in a world where punishment was rampant, we learned that responsibility should be dodged at all costs.

Being responsible *is not* the same as being at fault, rather it means you recognize that you have a choice, which is between doing what is *normal, easy, and destructive,* or doing what is *inconvenient, uncomfortable, and constructive.*

Can there be any issues with the element of Air itself?

With an abundance of the element of Air and a lack of Earth, we can feel floaty, and sometimes ungrounded. If this is a problem, doing grounding techniques to bring in Earth will anchor you to this world, without diminishing the higher experiences.

The element of Air does not lend itself to following the rules set by Fire which wants to be rising, dominating, burning up more territory. Those guided by universal love have no interest in playing by the rules, and those guided by higher levels of consciousness see through lies which others wouldn't question for fear of confrontation.

If you aim to live in a continuous state of being at one with everything within a material-reductionist culture, you're likely to get branded insane, or at least foolish:

"Give up learning and be free from all your troubles.

Must I fear what others fear?
Should I fear starvation
when there is abundance?
Should I fear darkness
when that light is shining everywhere?

Most people have too much;
I alone seem to be missing something.
Mine is indeed the mind of an ignoramus
in its unadulterated simplicity.
I am but a guest in this world.

While others rush about to get things done,
I accept what is offered.
I alone seem foolish,
earning little, spending less.
Other people strive for fame;
I avoid the limelight,
preferring to be left alone.

Indeed, I seem like an idiot:
no mind, no worries.
I drift like the waves of the sea.
Without direction, like the restless wind.

All people settle down in their grooves;
I alone am stubborn and remain outside.
But where I am most different from others is
in knowing I am nourished by the great Mother!"
~Lao Tzu, 20th verse Tao Te Ching

To balance the directionless and ineffectual aspects of Air, we can build more Earth and Fire. Building more Earth and Fire while activating Air is like filling a balloon up and tying it to the ground.

Earth, the part of us that is overmindful of the mundane day to day practicalities, that cannot see the big picture, is "lightened up," while the Air, that part of us that would be content to float from one blissed out experience to the next is given a boundary to work within, a direction. Without Earth, there's no reference.

Fire, which can be heartless and overzealous, has its unbridled passion turned toward higher aims, toward

118

aspirations for love and unity.

When you've experienced pain in close relationships in the past, which all of us have when you consider familial relations, you can become blocked by the toxic state of Water, preventing you from getting up into the Air, like a bird dipped in crude oil. So to be in the Air with *purity*, you must start to heal the wounds that keep your Heart sealed away, gradually becoming cleaner, lighter, and more open in an upward spiral.

There are those who believe they're living from the Heart, when in fact they're living from the fantasies and delusions of Water. The clue is to look for selfish, possessive, self-indulgent behaviour.

The key to self understanding, as always, is to observe your thoughts, feelings, bodily sensations, and actions. What do you practice? Where do you devote your time and energy? Are you able to trust and let things go when the time has come, or do you feel deprived, desirous, and clingy? Do you judge the level of deserving of others? Can you speak about those who have harmed you with compassion and understanding?

These are the kind of questions we must all ask ourselves, to stay moving in the upward direction, toward the Heart, toward our evolution.

The real difficulty is that you must confront the painful experiences and face your demons while standing in the light to make progress. Otherwise you're swimming in the swamp, pretending to be soaring, and practising nothing but mental masturbation.

Of course, we all deserve compassion for ourselves, forgiveness for the fact that we are born into a world with many rough edges, and kindness towards the calluses and scars that we've formed as a result.

Kindness, but not laziness or irresponsibility; not blaming those who have hurt us for our state, whatever that state may be, and valuing ourselves enough to not tolerate toxic behaviours.

You cannot rescue anyone, and you cannot help anyone who does not desire to be helped. To attempt to do so is to step on autonomy, to crush free will, which is a sacred gift granted to all sentient life.

This is one of the deeper meanings of "*turning the other cheek*" and it's one of the most difficult practices you may undertake. It relates to the deepest level of compassion: holding someone with kindness – or holding yourself – through a necessary suffering, a suffering which liberates.

Being overly fiery; self-centred (meeting one's needs by harming others), domineering, confrontational, attacking, controlling, and destructive, creates an insensitivity to Air.

In the same way that a wildfire sucks in huge volumes of oxygen, the element of Fire can fall into a state of, "Me, me, me!" And the focus becomes about gaining more and more material power, more and more dominance over others, not a gentle power from within.

Fortunately, this power can be redirected if that individual has an opening of the Heart, because of the energy of Fire which is always rising up. Instead of focusing on "rising up the ranks" in business for example, one may become focused on rising up in song, rising up in prayer, rising up in positive choices which make a difference in the lives around you.

There are many examples of CEO turned impassioned spiritual seeker, and those people can do a great deal of good because of the intense power and influence they wield, using it for the benefit of humanity rather than for lower aims. Many spiritual schools and healing centres have been funded and fostered by these kinds of people, so we must aim to support them in having an enlightening experience, rather than judging them for any negative actions.

This is especially true because of a false dichotomy that exists: the perception that there is an Us, and there is an external force called Them.

There is no Us-Vs-Them.

When we listen to those who have turned away from being elite power brokers and wielders of dark influence, a common story unfolds: those who appear to hold power are as trapped in the illusions of this world as everyone else. They don't control the power, it controls them, it is their addiction.

In general less than the 1% of the 1% of the 1%, are the "men behind the curtain", only a small handful of individuals. And, are they our enemy? No, they are *God wearing a villain's mask*, spurring the current evolution in consciousness and spirituality that is unfolding.

Fearing, being angry toward, or obsessing over them brings

no value to the world. Forgiving them, and abandoning the dominant paradigm from the deepest core of yourself, however, brings value to all beings.

Many people in the world are suffering from injustice, I'm in no position to tell you not to get angry at injustice; I get angry about injustice too.

At the end of the day, we can do more to create a just world by focusing our attention on *creating a just world* than we can by raging and blaming. We can make the crumbling old paradigm obsolete if we turn our attention to a just and sustainable future and walk toward it.

I share the following poem with you, which illustrates the pain and beauty which is involved in opening the heart. The image that comes to mind is of a clay pot breaking open so that it can let in the whole universe.

"*When love beckons to you, follow him,*
Though his ways are hard and steep.
And when his wings enfold you yield to him,
Though the sword hidden among his pinions may wound
you.
And when he speaks to you believe in him,
Though his voice may shatter your dreams
as the north wind lays waste the garden.

For even as love crowns you so shall he crucify you. Even as
he is for your growth so is he for your pruning.
Even as he ascends to your height and caresses your
tenderest branches that quiver in the sun,
So shall he descend to your roots and shake them in their
clinging to the earth.

Like sheaves of corn he gathers you unto himself.
He threshes you to make you naked.
He sifts you to free you from your husks.
He grinds you to whiteness.
He kneads you until you are pliant;
And then he assigns you to his sacred fire, that you may
become sacred bread for God's sacred feast.

All these things shall love do unto you that you may know
the secrets of your heart, and in that knowledge become a
fragment of Life's heart.
But if in your fear you would seek only love's peace and
love's pleasure,
Then it is better for you that you cover your nakedness and
pass out of love's threshing-floor,
Into the seasonless world where you shall laugh, but not all
of your laughter, and weep, but not all of your tears.
Love gives naught but itself and takes naught but from itself.
Love possesses not nor would it be possessed;
For love is sufficient unto love.

When you love you should not say, "God is in my heart," but
rather, "I am in the heart of God."
And think not you can direct the course of love, for love, if it
finds you worthy, directs your course.

Love has no other desire but to fulfil itself.
But if you love and must needs have desires, let these be your
desires:
To melt and be like a running brook that sings its melody to
the night.
To know the pain of too much tenderness.
To be wounded by your own understanding of love;

123

And to bleed willingly and joyfully.
To wake at dawn with a winged heart and give thanks for
another day of loving;
To rest at the noon hour and meditate love's ecstasy;
To return home at eventide with gratitude;
And then to sleep with a prayer for the beloved in your heart
and a song of praise upon your lips."
~Kahlil Gibran, On Love

Practices for Soaring in the Air

Because Air is the element which humanity has the hardest
time connecting with, it is the most difficult to nurture within
ourselves without focused practice.

It's ephemeral and invisible, easily dispersed, and until you've
flown nothing can adequately describe the bliss that being
enraptured in Air can bring you.

The fastest route to the elevated experiences of Air is through
selfless devotion. What you devote yourself to is entirely up
to you, here I offer a few suggestions.

You may mentor or care for a child. The unconditional love
associated with Air is said to be most like the love of a parent
for a child. I don't mean to suggest that you should have a
child, there are many children in need of love, probably many
in your neighbourhood or community.

How about offering selfless service and kindness to the old,
infirm, or dying, or volunteering in a palliative care unit?

You might support people in making a better life for
themselves, bringing comfort and assistance to impoverished

or disabled people.
Make sure that while you offer your selfless service,
regardless of the recipient, that you see those you're
supporting as exactly who they are: **You**, wearing a different
skin.

Focus on how easily you could be in their shoes if life had
dealt you a different hand, and thank the divine grace which
was kind to you in your life circumstances.

Let it be the same grace which moves you as a vehicle for
kindness, reducing suffering, and spreading compassion in
your community. Let the hand of Love guide your hand, and
let it be the drum which echoes in your heart.

Aside from being of service, you can also participate in
meditations for peace, compassion, and planetary wellbeing
for all beings. The meditation can be in the woods, a
monastery, or a church; the place doesn't matter. What
matters is that you're able to go deep inside yourself and see
the world being a more kind and gentle place for all life.

Devotional singing is a path that can lead straight into the
sky for some. Kirtan, choir, or Gregorian, again what is most
important is that it lights you up inside and takes you higher.

Within shamanic cultures that I've encountered, the path to
the sky has been through dance, physical austerity, and
plants.

While fasting is not for everyone, when I've done long fasts
and *earned my hunger* I've noticed that my focus has gone
completely to the divine, and as my body becomes physically
light, so do my thoughts and emotions. This austerity of food

is so common to the spiritual traditions of the world that it is nearly universal. Shamans, Buddhists, Hindus, Christians, Taoists; nearly every tradition that I know of has some practice of fasting and it is not a coincidence.

Whether it's Ecstatic Dance, 5 Rhythms Dance, a simple hypnotic shuffle, or the Sun Dance, ritual dance can induce a high level of consciousness and spiritual connection.

Finally, working with the plant teachers. I've seen how profoundly Abuelita can sweep one's heart clean, and with sincere desire to heal I've seen even the most cynical person floating on a cloud after spending some time with her. The plant teachers offer so much because they show us what we can achieve if we clear away the trauma, and then they *help us to clear it away*. They give us an intention, and they give us the tools to get there.

Out of these practices, it's my sincere hope that you can find at least one which resonates with you. There are many paths to the heart, may you find yours.

For an advanced and intensely challenging ritual of transformation, see the Air Ritual for Soaring in the Astral Wind on page 179.

Your ultimate intention for the Air element is to release all goals; to enter into a state of Ayni; right relationship and reciprocity; accept all of life as the sky accepts the clouds.

How Trauma Affects the Elements

Earth is the element which connects us to the outer world, and when we experience trauma, we often associate it with the outer world since the harm is coming from "out there".

Traumatic experiences tell you that Earth is not a safe place to live, that your *body* is not a safe place to live. So your consciousness is pushed higher, but not in a positive way, not with a healthy foundation.

As many ascetics have, we *escape*. Not because we're enraptured by grace, but because the present circumstances are hellish or unbearable. In any spiritually centred community, you will encounter individuals who are there to escape themselves, rather than find themselves.

As Earth relates to our physical health, trauma often leads to poor wellbeing in the body. For example, those with a strong connection to Earth often have more physical mass and a more dense structure, which is completely normal. Yet those same people may develop obesity if their Earthy constitution is combined with significant life trauma. Through studies of the effects of adverse childhood experiences, the connection between trauma and obesity is becoming well defined.

Obesity is only one example; the underlying effect of trauma on Earth and our relationship with the body is fear, hatred, and disgust for the physical self.
Each person expresses these themes differently and uniquely. Cutting, anorexia, high risk activities which may damage the

body, and ultimately suicide can be seen as ways in which damage to one's connection with Earth (and with the body) can play out.

Tattoos, piercing, excessive cosmetic surgery, "roid-monkeys", and similar body dysmorphic activities can stem from the desire to reclaim the body from traumatic or disempowering events or circumstances.

Out of the four basic elements, **Water** is the one most strongly and obviously impacted by trauma.

How this shows up most commonly is lethargic energy levels and toxic stagnation throughout the being.
Common expressions of trauma through the view of the Water element are depression, anxiety, addiction, mental confusion, mental illness, chronic fatigue and in general a lack of *joie de vivre*. Mental illnesses where fantasy or paranoia overcome reality are especially common in the case of severe trauma.

In the best case scenario, since Water is the element of imagination and creativity trauma can lead to the creation of great artists such as Vincent van Gogh and Edvard Munch. Art is Water's way of expressing and pouring out the pain.

When faced with trauma, **Fire** is most commonly extinguished. In cases where it's not, it can burn the victim up inside and turn them into abusers themselves. Because they feel dominated and powerless, they turn to dominating and attempting to take the power of others. But, it never works because personal power can only ever come from within, meaning that their drive to abuse is insatiable. This is the realm of torturers and psychopaths, though not all

128

psychopaths have experienced trauma. "*An eye for an eye*" perfectly describes the reaction of Fire to trauma: you burned me, now I'm going to burn you. In less common examples, the element of Fire may react like this, "You think you hurt me? Just watch, I'm going to overcome you and be better than you will ever be."

This "Screw you, just watch!" attitude can result in that person overcoming the trauma, or it may just result in a narcissistic and overcompensating personality. This is the birthing place of delusions of grandeur.

Trauma impacts **Air** by "clipping its wings". As Fire and Air are the more dynamic elements, they are impacted in a similar way; they are turned off. In a person who is dominant in Air, they will most commonly unhinge from the world in a polarization of those who are dominant in Earth. The result is a total lack of awareness of the functioning of the external world. In other words, dissociation.

The difference between the mental illnesses which are influenced by Water versus Air are that with Water, the view of the world is skewed, while with Air the connection to reality is diminished or entirely severed.

Consciousness

Building Consciousness and practising concentration of the mind keeps us safe while building willpower, opening the heart, and going beyond to the realm of Spirit. Consciousness is the best solution to the directionless floating of Air.

This is where our story takes a heady turn; it's natural that you may need to read and re-read the concepts presented in this section. If you take the time to practice and integrate what I share with you here, *I promise that your spiritual practice will transform your entire world.*

Consciousness is not an element in the way you would normally think of elements, though it's a force which is one of the foundations of the manifest universe. It is not a physical element, rather it is the blueprint or governor for the physical elements and their interrelated interactions. In the same way that our DNA is the blueprint for the structures of our bodies, consciousness is the blueprint for the universe.

It is the force which directs all others within you, and it allows you to move energies and change states of mind within yourself. With Consciousness you can bring positive energies in, and then expel and release energy which no longer serves you.

Ultimately, it allows you to reimagine and rewrite yourself, redraw your internal Map of Reality to be more harmonious and in alignment with macrocosmic truths.

Strengthening the Mind

Sometimes you might think, "My mind is so busy, so slippery; my ego is so strong. Why would I want to make my mind *stronger*?"

You strengthen the mind for exactly this reason: these are symptoms of a mind that's been weakened by a culture designed to keep you from thinking.

School teaches you that learning is difficult and boring, and that knowledge is passed down by a source of higher authority, rather than something to be explored and directed by your own internal compass of curiosity and imagination.

All mammals, humans included, learn best by playing and exploring in a non-structured environment. The dominant culture suppresses this highly creative aspect of the lower self, and so it comes out in shadow forms such as war, shame, and violent pornography. When the lower self is fully engaged in uninhibited play and creativity, the mind can enter into a state of calm flow.

When you have an intensely distracted monkey mind, difficulty concentrating, and obsessive or unavoidable thoughts, this reflects the need to strengthen and train your mind.

You are taught to think in linear terms, "Once I have a strong body, then I'll get emotionally clean, and then I'll be more dynamic and wilful, then I'll be able to love, and then I'll be able to concentrate..." It's true that the *focus* must be on one or two areas at a time, to concentrate your efforts, but how long can you sustain your focus? Until you have built a foundation through repeated practice, no effort can be sustained for long.

You can use the ADD nature of your conditioning to your advantage; by spending only 5-20 minutes on a practice, the monkey mind doesn't have time to get as bored or distracted or as intensely uncomfortable. Once years have been invested in building your concentration of the mind, then it's valuable to spend a month or more focusing on building just one quality.

In dark, judgmental moments, you might worry and experience anxiety, and then accept the label of "control freak", but **anxiety and worry are not control: they are fear and attachment**.

What is Attachment?

You're seeking control because we're all so fundamentally lacking in it, but we don't know what control *really* is, so we settle for attachment, founded in judgment, pessimism, cynicism and so on. Control is something that comes from within, and is directed exclusively within yourself.

Nothing external can be controlled, and in truth you can only control one thing at all: your mind. Your soul controls your mind, and your mind controls everything else within your experience of life, because *it is the mind that generates your experience of life through the senses.*

Your mind is literally the interface between your soul, meaning *you*, and the material world via your body. The stronger your mind is, the more easily you can manipulate your experience of the material world, and the more the insubstantial and impermanent nature of your reality is revealed.

Specifically for our practice, concentration of the mind is essential. This is because we engage in a process that rapidly and dramatically expands the mind, yet only with *controlled expansion* of the mind do we reap the most vital long term rewards.

To get to the treasure requires putting yourself in an uncomfortable position for a length of time, while you adjust to seeing things from a new and different perspective.

How do you train the mind? The best way is through a daily meditation practice where you focus the mind and continuously bring it back to a point of clarity. You may find that after training the mind, that your journeys become deeper and more clear.

A substantial part of the spiritual path regardless of tradition follows a nearly universal theme: achieving detachment. Dissolving attachment and strengthening the concentration of the mind are the primary intentions of working with the element of Consciousness. Plant medicine work is particularly effective in this aim, since it can rapidly demonstrate that you are not your body, not your feelings, and not your mind.

Why is this theme so central? Because attachments to people, objects, and perspectives **hide the pain of loss**, and the pain of loss is one of the primary tools of the ego. It's that part of us that hangs on to stories and tells us we're separate from all we perceive.

Confronting Pain and Identity

When you attempt to release attachment this can trigger repressed pain, which offers you an opportunity for deep for healing through grieving. Detachment from the mind is often considered the final level, and we can ease ourselves into this understanding through practising meditation.

There are intensive forms of meditation which facilitate the process of detachment. For example, focusing on components of your body, such as a toenail, and localize your consciousness there, and then withdraw it again, stating, "I am not my toenail" and so on, moving through the whole body.

Our aim is building strong concentration of the mind in general, so at the end of this section I will share with you one simple and effective meditation you can do at home.

The practice of **acknowledging** is a simple and effective technique for building detachment and concentration of the mind through everyday life:

When you feel bliss, say, "Bliss, bliss, bliss."

When you hear something that distracts you from whatever activity you are engaged in, say, "Hearing, hearing, hearing."

When you pick something up, say, "Touching, touching, touching."

When the monkey mind takes over the show, say, "Thinking, thinking, thinking." Pain: "Pain, pain, pain." Pleasure: "Pleasure, pleasure, pleasure." and so on.

Whatever phenomenon happens, you are acknowledging it, acknowledging the mental process of recognition, which rapidly builds concentration and detachment.

By disidentifying from and removing yourself from the reaction to the sensations of the world, you can go much deeper into them.

Detachment and concentration of the mind lead to some important outcomes, such as being able to observe your mind and your behaviour for negative patterns emerging. You can then use your willpower and self-love to correct the negative patterns.

If you cannot see your reactions or your thoughts as they emerge, you will not be able to see the chain of beliefs that form your thought patterns and ultimately your choices.

The process follows:

Awareness ➡ Choice ➡ Choosing

First you gain awareness by detaching from the immediacy of your environment, which leads to the understanding that everything you do, every little motion, every breath, is a choice. Once you understand that in each and every moment you have unlimited choices, you then begin to choose more and more consciously, and in time it becomes a habit.

For example, this is how I discovered meditation in my childhood:

"I was lying in my mother's bed watching TV and noticed

that I had to pee. I didn't want to take the time to go and pee, so I continued to watch in a zombified state.

Suddenly I realized that I no longer had to pee. Shocked, I tried to figure out why and vaguely remembered that in fact I had gone to the washroom during the commercial break without the slightest conscious choice. I had stood up, walked several meters, relieved myself, and returned without a single thought, and this disturbed me.

So with the best awareness I could muster as a child, I turned off the TV and stood up slowly, moving each muscle by choice one at a time. I made the full walking motion while moving even the tiniest muscles by choice, leaving nothing to the subconscious mind.

From then on, I started making time to sit on a large concrete pillar outside and be as present as I could. I didn't want to be on autopilot, didn't want some hidden force to direct me. I wanted to be in control of myself."

I had no idea what meditation was at the time, or that what I was doing would later lead me to practice Vipassanā meditation, but I was inspired by the interplay between conscious action and unconscious action.

Your Map of Reality

What if you could be anyone? What if your reality could look like anything? The truth is that the boundaries and limitations of your present day reality are all written on a map that you made long, long ago.

This is one of the ultimate intentions of detachment and concentration of the mind. To build your awareness and ability to choose to the point where you can rewrite your map of reality.

Most of the time what you see as reality is a thin veil woven by the ego to normalize the conditions you were raised in, and to help you navigate the world around you. Even after years of digging and rewriting, most of us can only reach the tip of the iceberg of the subconscious, the depth and complexity of which is incomprehensible by the conscious mind.

Where does this map come from? Let's say that as a child your parents were unsupportive of your creativity, and instead expected you to be quiet and get good marks in school.

Without even knowing it, these conditions become imprinted not as,
"*my parents* are oppressive and smothering."
but instead, "**the world** is oppressive and smothering."

This is why it's so critically important that we change the world "from the inside out" because more often than not the world is just fine, and what is disharmonious is our *perception* of the world.

With an unconsciously defined view of reality, our subconscious will go to great lengths to prove this view to be **right**, even if it tells you terrible things about yourself.

The subconscious *wants* the map to be *real*, and so it unconsciously attract situations which confirm our beliefs about the world, it seeks evidence. As long as it can make the map appear to be the territory, the beliefs are thought to be true and continue unquestioned, assumed to be unwavering truths.

One method for building awareness on this level, is to listen to what you say about, "the world." For example, "**The world is so unjust!**"

After becoming aware of a statement like this, first notice elements of the world which are *not* that way. Is a flower harsh? Is a maple leaf harsh? Is a warm spring breeze harsh?

Secondly, ask yourself, "I see that the world appears
_____, how does that correlate to what my parents said to me or demonstrated to me about the world?"
Were my parents harsh? Did they tell me that the world was harsh? Was a teacher or other source of authority harsh with me?

In this way you can dig into *where your beliefs come from*. Almost all of your beliefs form this way, and they are not consciously or rationally chosen. As you unwind the structure of your belief systems, you may start to realize that what you think of as you is actually just a bunch of fingers pointing to beliefs which were never yours to begin with. The ego says, "I'm a person who believes in X, Y, Z, 1, 4, and 7, but not A, B, or C!"

It creates a complex array of *I do believe this and not that* type of statements. But if you haven't examined those beliefs, haven't thought them through to their conclusion, how can you know if they're really *yours*?

Here's a simple exercise for you right now: with a pen and paper, begin to write, "**I believe**". Write every belief that comes into your mind without judgment. The *without judgment* part is key here, because if you're judging what you instinctively want to write you're only hiding from yourself to guard your ego.

Maybe you'll find some beliefs embarrassing, maybe you'll even be ashamed to admit a few of them. Maybe you'll cringe at a couple and say, "I don't want to believe this any more, *I know it's not even true*, but my gut reaction is to believe it."

Let yourself write uninterrupted in a stream of consciousness. Give it 30 minutes. If you get stuck, keep writing the same things over and over. Believe me, it would take you *weeks* to write out all of your beliefs if you could access them all. This will scratch the surface, and teach you about how your mind organizes its beliefs, and which ones it guards from you to keep you out of the mental control room.

Giving and Taking

Tibetan Buddhism is a union of ancient Buddhism (Mahayana), Tantra (Vajrayana) and shamanism (called Bön in modern times).

The practice of Tonglen, which means *Giving and Taking*, may have roots in the tantric and shamanic practices of Tibetan Buddhism, and is a practice which offers a short and direct path to greater internal freedom. I'll show you how to use it to integrate a journey, but you can use it to heal the source of almost any negative emotion; it is a pair of tweezers, which you can use to pluck thorns.

Tonglen is a practice of short term pain, long term gain. It's a process where we take what's chaotic and settle it with kindness. This is a practice of **learning by doing**, and so rather than giving you a lot of theory, I invite you to practice. Download the guided audio version of Tonglen from the Journeying website here: http://journeying.ca/meditations

To begin, take a moment and journal about something that you touched on in your last journey which was challenging. Something that you feel upset or triggered about when you remember it. Alternatively, you can use an intrusive or disturbing thought or memory from any point in your life, but don't pick the worst thing, just something *mildly* uncomfortable.

After taking some time to write about it; what you remember, the mix of emotions that it brings up for you, how it feels in your body, what it reminds you of from your life, and how you have interpreted your own identity through the lens of this experience... then find a comfortable place to meditate.

In the comfortable place – such as the edge of a chair or a meditation bench – sit with your spine straight, your tailbone slightly curved forward, your chin gently tucked.

Imagine a vine rooted at the base of your spine which connects straight up into the sky, and imagine it lengthening your spine. Then, relax all unnecessary muscles in your body. Take three deep breaths and allow your muscles to turn to melted butter on the exhalation.

In this state of relaxation, offer the benefits of this meditation to the ancestors, to the descendants, and to the benefit of all beings.

Now, seated with your eyes closed, bring that memory which you journaled about to mind. Notice your aversion to it, notice wanting to run away from the unpleasantness, notice how it feels in your body.

As you visualize your subject, breathe these feelings and sensations in deeply. Accept what you see as it arises, don't attempt to change it in any way.

Breathe it into your body in a deep, slow breath. First breathing and expanding into your belly, then your chest, then your collar bone area, completely expanding your lungs.

When your lungs are completely full, begin to slowly breathe out, and as you visualize the event and the people involved, send them positive feelings. Send them love, kindness, acceptance, and forgiveness.

Do this until your lungs are completely empty, and then start again, breathing in the darkness and pain of that event. Repeat this cycle for about 5 minutes.

As you become more practised, the technique will quickly become second nature to you, which will allow you to focus more and more on the fundamental practice, which is breathing in (or taking) what is difficult, and breathing out (giving) relief. As you practice the cycle of darkness transforming into lightness, you'll find that the event has less and less of a charge, less and less sting.

After the event has been neutralized – it may regain its charge as deeper levels of emotion rise – you may complete the meditation by meditating on the bright thought of unobstructed clear white light for a few minutes.

What Does It All Mean?

A brief summary of our intentions up to this point:
- Cleanse and heal your **body.**
- Purify and connect with your **emotions** and reduce both triggering and numbness.
- Build a strong and integral **will**.
- Open your **heart** to seeing the interconnectedness of all things.
- Strengthen and expand the **mind**.
- Connect with the **Creator**.

All of these are best done in parallel, as *they are all complimentary.*

Where you need to place your focus will be different than for someone else. Some of us have healthy bodies but are numb to our emotions, some of us are angry and have a closed heart, and so on.

Our immediate larger intention as a species is opening and empowering the heart, and in doing so we inevitably confront many dark corners of ourselves.

It is that darkness which has obscured your light; your light source hits blockages and shadows are cast. We must purge the blockages from the pipes so that we can see with clarity, see without fear, to find the ultimate treasure.
To this end, our ceremonial practices – aligning with and building internal energies, meditation, self inquiry, and working with plant medicine – can strongly support us. But we must take the steps in front of us, we must have the courage to walk the path.

Post-Ceremony Integration

The week after a ceremony represents the merging of the spiritual work with our everyday reality, and is equally as important as the ceremony itself.

After a "spiritual surgery", we must take this period of convalescence to support the healing. Think of yourself as having invisible stitches for 10 days.
The ceremony will "close" 10 days after leaving the ceremonial space, and until then the work continues in full force on the subtle planes. After that, the integration and inner work continue for a lifetime.

Pay attention to what life brings you during this time frame, how you are being tested and rewarded, blessed and cleansed.

This is an important time to cover a piece of theory:
You have given up many beliefs which you thought were the truth.

You are now in a state of **feeling** everything which those beliefs protected your from, and needing to be **discerning** rather than operating from imposed morality. You are being presented with opportunities to see **reality**, rather than filtering your experience through imposed belief systems.

In this time, you will likely experience pendulum swings of mood and behaviour patterns, and may feel that you're going crazy and acting strangely.

In time, to the extent which you allow yourself to keep feeling, and making "mistakes" (think of the image of a baby falling down while learning to walk) you will find your new rhythm and new balance, and in those liberated areas live based on your own compass and your own values, from your soul and your authenticity, rather than the ones that were imposed on you dogmatically from your family, society, and religion of origin.

We often feel our lives are "in control", when in fact they are tied up in these rigidly held moralizing belief systems. These moralities resonate with the world of Water, and the baby soul stage, and are outdated modes of operating which no longer serve. They are all of the old world belief systems, the old paradigm, and tend to react very strongly when touched upon. What does this look like?

The ego distracts with fear, and worry, which may feel like control. You may even be tempted to call yourself a "control freak" if you worry often.

These beliefs are deeply ingrained in our painful experiences of early childhood, and when we touch on them we can experience feelings of identifying with those painful experiences.

In other words, when pain is triggered by, for example, perceived abandonment, some part of you may identify with that pain and attempt to convince you that it "is you" rather than simply an experience you are having.

Instead of saying, "I experienced distance between myself and another" the inner voice of the ego whispers, "I'm unworthy of love."

This stems from a biological imprinting system of the body, where we are incapable of seeing our parents and caregivers as less than perfect under a certain age.

So if a father harms their child, the child's mind won't internalize the message, "**My father is** abusive and unbalanced." But instead, "**I must have** done something wrong. Better watch out next time."

This is because the child's mind believes their models are perfect by default. This extends to the level of society as well. If a mother is neglectful of their child, instead of thinking, "My mother has exceeded her coping skills." instead the child is likely to believe, "I'm not good enough for my mother to love me."

When you behave in opposition to these beliefs, you may experience an anxious voice saying, "*I've got to do this! Or _____ will happen and I'll die! I'll lose approval! I'll lose power, and money!* **They'll see who I really am***!*"

In other words, the ego causes an intense fear of loss when we attempt to change these foundations of the identity, foundations of false personality, our map of reality. It points to the painful event, and says, "That's you! You better keep playing along, or everyone else will see who you really are, and then what will they think?"

Of course, who you "really are" is not the painful event, but a fragment of Divine Consciousness, but in those moments it can be difficult to remember this fact.

So, what can you do about it?

You can affirm, "I don't know, and cannot know anything. The only valid way of judging my behaviour is by assessing the effects and results of my actions, again and again over time. Outward appearances are an illusion, I choose to see my world with depth."

Whenever you do something, or see someone else doing something which you're uncertain about, you can ask, "What are the effects of their/my behaviour?"

After that, **continue feeling and evaluating**.
Keep in mind the catch with this: when pressing against deeply held beliefs, the "outcome" might be feeling gripped with fear of death, and massive emotional, and even physical discomfort. This is where we must remember:
"Each moment I feel discomfort, is a moment I'm healing and growing."

In general, being connected with your body is a great way of discerning the truth.

To summarize and simplify:
Keep feeling, keep a "don't know mind", let it be OK to feel crazy, and evaluate the effects of your choices based on their outcomes rather than moralizations or emotional reactions of yourself or others. Keep feeling your body, keep feeling your emotions. Seek support and connection.

Some other integrative practices you can look into, to see if they're right for you:
- Being in the sun, warming your body.
- Acupuncture and massage.

- Smudging yourself and your home with sage, cedar, and frankincense.
- Tonglen and the other meditations and rituals included in this book.
- Working with or wearing a stone during a ceremony, and then using it as an object to remind you of the insights you gained.
- Getting together with someone else from the ceremony who you feel safe with, either on the phone or in person, to talk about your experiences.
- Continuing to follow the dieta, both the physical diet, and the emotional and spiritual components.
- Taking a warm bath with Epsom salts and essential oils.
- Start a garden, get your hands dirty. Indoors in pots, if that's what you can manage, but preferably directly connected to the Earth.
- Go for a walk in nature, preferably to a high and dry place.
- Listen to positive music which uplifts your spirits.
- You may look into the supplements 5-HTP and St. John's wort. Citicoline and Pantethine, or the Milner Acetylcholine Protocol can have positive effects in some people recovering from PTSD. Of course, *this is not a recommendation to take these supplements*, simply to bring them to your attention so that you can do your own research, and see if they would be helpful to you.

During the time after the ceremony, you will likely find yourself confronted with old addictive patterns, urges, and behaviours.

Why do we experience addiction? Because we're numbing out pain and reducing stress, either physical or existential, but more often than not existential. And I don't just mean drugs and alcohol; sex addiction, video game addiction, gambling addiction, workaholism, addiction to a specific emotional state (anxiety, rage, fear, self-pity, martyrdom), and so on.

They are all dopamine stimulating behaviours that gloss over and numb out the pain of a desolate, lonely, and painful past, and soothes feelings of existential crisis.

They reduce the heavy burden of stress that we carry, and help us cope with life, even though we know they entail serious negative consequences for our health. In short, **addiction is a surrogate for connection**.

When you go inside yourself, you can follow the trail of emotion back to the cause, back to the source, and release it. Doing this before, after, and during a ceremony can also speed up the healing process, by actively removing layers of emotional damage and unfelt pain.

You may then ask, "*So why doesn't everyone do this work?*" The originating, causal pain is strongly attached to identity, which is the foundation of false personality; the primary vehicle of expression of the ego. In other words, giving up the old pain is massively threatening to your ego, personality, and self-image!

Without tools or support, touching these areas, these "danger zones" of the psyche, can be one of the most terrifying and agonizing experiences we can know.

148

Why?

The mind functions in a way that normalizes everything around us, all of the toxic circumstances of our world. It wants to keep the roots of its control well hidden just as a tree wants to keep its roots hidden from animals that would damage them. The root of control of the ego is deep existential pain, and identification with that pain.

Old, deep, pain.

So when you follow the leaves (triggered emotions and disproportionate responses) back to the roots (early childhood pain experienced with existential crisis and fear of death) you threaten the core of who you have believed you are, because for most of your life the ego has been pointing at this pain and saying, "*This is you! Play nice, or I'll show everyone who you really are!*"

However, *it's a lie*. It's just a scary puppet show. Who you truly are is far, far greater than that.

Once you dig up the pain and release it, you're giving birth to your true self.

Of course, this isn't a "one shot deal." It's a deep, potentially life-long journey.

The good news is that with each stage, with every time that you show up with courage and a shovel and announce, "*Let's get digging!*" It becomes easier, more comfortable, less demolishing.

Why? Because each time you do it, you have more of yourself. Your true self. And once you have even an infinitesimal drop of your true self uncovered, you will understand why the Sufis call it the Pearl Beyond Price.

We all contain aspects of brokenness and wholeness, and so much of what we do as humans is done to conceal our brokenness. Once the wounds are covered, they fester and kills us.

Following a path of inner work triggers the old trauma, loosens it, and brings it to the light to be released. We offer up all of what we are to the light, for what no longer serves us to be burned up and turned to ashes that will rise, purify, and return to the earth to fertilize it.

In this way we don't need to hide from our brokenness anymore, but give it back to its originating source, which is the same source as wholeness. We offer it up, and ask for grace. When we practice this path we're saying to the boogie men in the basement, "*I'm not afraid of you any more, here I am! Come stand in the light!*"

With cleansing and transformation, and working with the spirits of plants – under guidance, and in a safe space with intention, we depersonalize and deidentify with the pain, and this makes the process so much easier, and so much faster.

In a three day retreat, it's reasonable to expect to uncover what would take you 20 years to uncover in a traditional talk-therapy setting, because we have tools of opening, uncovering, and releasing what they do not have access to. And that's not just my opinion, but the opinion of prominent doctors and psychiatrists.

This perspective of integrating pain will, I hope, help you to surrender to waves of emotion as they rise, rather than distracting from, stuffing, or redirecting them. My heart hopes that you will, in those painful moments of choice, step through the shadows in your emotions, rather than away from them.

Focus on light and love, but ***do not get lost*** dancing in the dazzling lights while your shadows and self-destructive patterns run and ruin your life. Follow the light to the clear, unobstructed place where compassion and kindness will help you to feel, and to forgive yourself. Then take that light, and shine it into the corners where the pain has been hiding.

Elemental Shamanic Rituals

Now we dive into deeper, more involved shamanic rituals.

These are powerful rituals, not to be taken lightly. If performed in a good and humble way, they will align you with powerful forces. The forms of these ceremonies are older than writing. They speak deeply to your blood, your subconscious, and your soul.

I say the *forms*, because I am not trying to make you into a Magyar Táltos, or a Native American, or anything else. These rituals are not from any one tradition, nor are they New Age. They could be called revivalist neo-shamanic, because they are ancient forms with room for us to create new traditions within.

A great struggle unfolded inside me as I sat to meditate on these rituals and prepare to release them from the esoteric, into the exoteric. There are subtle secrets hidden within these practices, keys to doorways that have been intentionally obscured. When you practice them in a focused, relaxed, and open state, profound shifts will take place inside of you that will radiate out through your life.

Remember that **you are the crucible**, the cauldron; magic happens by acting first with your body, then your emotions, then your mind, then your soul. Then the effects happen in reverse!

The ancestors rejoice when we take this time to listen to them, and the descendants are blessed by the chance to live in a better way than we do, the chance to have a closer connection with the Earth and with Spirit. Speak your prayers out loud for all of the worlds to hear.

While performing these rituals, until you are familiar with them, I recommend that you do not improvise. Before you deviate from what I'm about to share with you, get comfortable with the practice. If you are a shamanic practitioner with experience then I lay them at your feet, and leave it in the hands of your guides and ancestors. Otherwise, stay to the safe and well travelled roads.

You have my permission to share these rituals with anyone you choose to, as they're more powerful when performed in a group. All I ask is that you share the source of the ritual with them so that they are aware of the origins of what they're practising.

If this is uncharted territory for you and you are completely new to shamanic practice, the rituals may feel overwhelming, difficult, or forced. If you're stuck in your head and over-analyzing then there will be no juice, no soul in the rituals. Emotion is the fuel that drives these rituals deep into your being.

If you get stuck, look for local shamanic groups in your area and participate in their ceremonies. Remember that they will vary widely from group to group: trust your gut.

Prepare the Ritual

Before you begin, before you do anything to prepare, before any action arises, take a moment of silent reflection and **give away** the ritual to Spirit. Give away your ego, that part of you that thinks it's separate and unique. Give away the outcomes of the ritual, and let them be whatever they will be. Give away the benefits of the ritual to all beings everywhere, and to Spirit.

Each of the rituals I'm about to share with you has an element and a spirit which guide it. When the time comes during your preparation, give the ritual away to that spirit. Give away your belief that there's a "right way" and a "wrong way", and allow yourself to be present with the experience as it unfolds.

You are just one point in time, like a needle on a vinyl record that is spiralling around and around. The ancestors are the record before us, and the descendants are yet to be recorded. Give away the ritual for everyone who has come before you, and everyone who comes after.

Once you've given away the ritual, you can begin to "**set the stage**". Gather any materials you need, find a beneficial time to perform the ritual such as a lunar or solar event (New moon, full moon, equinox, solstice, etc.), and find a suitable place to perform the ritual where you will not be disturbed. Be sure to eat and drink before the ritual, as you should never eat during a ritual unless you are eating an offering as part of the ritual.

Once the time has come and you're preparing the ritual space, begin by focusing again on your giveaway, re-centred on letting go of any attachment to the ritual and giving away all of it to Spirit. Each ritual has a specific colour of clothing to wear.

Create a containing **space of protection** that will act as a boundary between the inner ritual space and the outer world. Create the boundary with stones, a chalk line, or a rope/string. While you create the physical boundary, ask the beneficial spirits of the land to hold the space and allow only positive influences into the ritual space. Within each ritual, I will suggest a shape for the boundary and a material to use.

Open the Ritual

In each of the rituals, when you see *open the ritual*, follow this section.

Once your boundary is created, cleanse it using smoke. Camphor, sage, frankincense, myrrh, copal, Palo Santo, pine or cedar resin are all good, or any other cleansing plant spirit that you work with. A burning charcoal disk in a bowl or seashell is ideal as a heat source, as you can add more incense to it as the ritual continues (these are sometimes called hookah charcoal). Take safety precautions whenever working with fire. I will also suggest specific incense for each ritual.

After cleansing the space with smoke, cleanse each participant, blowing the smoke slowly over them from toe to head, then again on their back side. You can use feathers, a bundle of leaves, hands, or breath for the smudging. Then cleanse each object and offering that will be used in the ritual, to purge them of any negative influences.

Begin by announcing your full name aloud, so that all of the spirits present know you, your family, and your bloodlines. This is how they know you're listening to them; they are always listening to you. Speak the family names of any bloodlines or ancestors you want to work.

Request patience and help in being humble, tell the spirits that you're young and still learning these ways. Even grey haired elders say this. We're *all* young and inexperienced.

Next, give thanks to the elements, directions, and spirits. When giving thanks, it's important to express gratitude for what *you* are grateful for. I will offer some ideas about the symbolism, but the emotion must come from within you. There is no universally true association between the directions and the elements. Think about it for a moment, from where you are:

- Which direction are the **mountains**?
- Which direction has the largest **body of water**?
- Which offers the most **heat from the Sun**?
- Which direction do the **prevailing winds** come from?

Someone living in Hungary will have a completely different answer from someone living in Thailand, and so on. You must figure this out for yourself. If you're uncertain, sit and meditate on it, while asking your ancestors for guidance.

Briefly:

- **Earth** is for life, vitality, nurturing.
- **Water** is for cleansing, sensuality, surrender.
- **Fire** is for warmth, courage, passion.
- **Air** is for wisdom, compassion, perspective.
- *Each element provides its own life-giving qualities.*

While giving thanks, hold on to a musical instrument such as a drum, rattle, bell, or chime. After each direction before turning to the next, sound your instrument for a moment.

Begin by facing **East**, and thank the spirit of the East for all that it brings to us humans. East is the direction of the sunrise, of Spring, of that which is constantly renewed. Every day that the sun rises, we have another opportunity to live in a good way. Give thanks for the element which you relate to the East (from your current location), expressing your appreciation for the qualities it brings to your life.

Turn to the **South**. In the Northern hemisphere, the South is where the sun spends most of its time and is the direction of Summer. This is a place of growth and fecundity, of play and long days, of being with tribe and family out in the world. After saying your thanks, offer thanks for the element which you associate with the South.

Turn to the **West**. The West is the place where everything goes to rest, of the Autumn, where this world passes by into the next. This is the place of letting go, of grief, and of mystery. This is the quiet place where everything is resolved in its dissolution. Offer thanks for the element you associate with the West.

Turn to the **North**. This is the place of quiet reflection, of Winter, of subtle tasks done indoors, of darkness and closeness, of deep dreams. This is where seeds rest and wait for the warmth to return, and in their patience come to know themselves. Offer thanks for the element you associate with the North.

Turn to the **Earth**. Without our Mother, nothing is possible for us humans. Even when our hair turns grey, we're still tiny infants cradled in her bosom. She has endless kindness and unconditional love for us, and she wants to teach us how to live in a good way. Consider the profound gift that life on Earth is, and then express your thanks.

Turn to the **Sky**. The sky is the vast source of cosmic wisdom, from where all dreams and knowledge descend. In the same way that humans and other animals would have nowhere to live without Earth, the Earth would have nowhere to live without the manifest universe, the vast and infinite expanse.

Thank any other **spirits** that you're working with in the ritual you're performing.

Thank the **spirits of the land** that you are on, ask them to not obstruct your ritual, and to receive whatever benefit they can from it.

Thank **the people** who have traditionally inhabited the land, all of the **plants** that you will be working with during the ritual, your **teachers and elders**, the **ancestors**, the **Creator**, and **All that Is**.

Once you've finished giving thanks and you feel full of gratitude, state your **intention**. Why are you doing this? What positive effect are you intending to generate? How will that outcome make the world a more harmonious place, and how will it align you with the forces of harmony?

Once you have stated your intention, you're now ready to begin the ritual for the specific intention you've chosen.

Earth Ritual for Rooted Strength

This ritual is best done in a place in nature where you will go frequently, as an ongoing practice that will ground you and connect you with the Earth element on an ongoing basis.

A suitable place may be on a private piece of land, deep in a public forest, or on a farm which you have access to.

Materials needed:
- 20 meters of strong string, preferably hemp, for the boundary.
- 1 patch of cloth per participant, preferably white or yellow, 10 centimetres square.
- An equal number of short sections of string, about 10 centimetres in length.
- Pine and/or cedar resin with frankincense.
- A charcoal disk with holder for burning resins.
- A lighter.
- Earth tone coloured clothing.

Here's an overview of the ritual
- Gather materials, dress in Earth tone colours.
- Find a location for the ritual.
- Give away the outcomes to Mother Earth.
- Create a square boundary with the long string.
- *Open the ritual.*
- Connect with a stone and a plant.
- Harvest a leaf.
- Smell the leaf and the stone.
- Listen.

- Hold the stone and the leaf over the smoke in your right hand, the cloth and the string in your left.
- Speak your intentions again with emotion.
- Listen to your body, feel how it reacts.
- Place the stone and leaf into the cloth and add a few of your eyelashes.
- Tie up the prayer tie to the boundary.
- Conclude by giving thanks 3 times and cracking your knuckles.
- Perform each full Moon and new Moon.
- Journal about improvements in Earth energy between rituals.

Begin by giving away the ritual and its outcomes to Mother Earth. She is the spirit we work with in this ritual.

Once you have a suitable spot chosen, one you know you will have access to over a long period of time, spend time walking around in this place, some time just being and observing. When you go there, dress in Earth tone colours.

Find a stone with a flat top, preferably at least as large as your head; a boulder at waist height is ideal. This stone will be your altar. With the altar at the centre, take your string and create a large square around the area with sides of equal length (*about 5 meters or 5 paces per side*), forming the protective barrier. Tie the string above your head through trees, or on tall dead branches inserted into the ground. It's important that the string is high enough up that no one will walk into it and damage it in between your visits. **Tie it tightly as it will support the prayer ties.** Alternatively, the prayer ties can be tied to branches within the ritual space. Once the boundary string is in place, *open the ritual* as described above. Place the charcoal disk in its holder at the centre of the alter, and periodically add more plant resin to it as you feel called to throughout the ritual.

Take some time to move through the ritual space, and find a small stone that you are instinctively drawn to. Ask the stone to help you build Earth energy inside of yourself, and ask for its permission to move it. Wait for the response as a feeling in your body, a feeling of "This feels ok." or "This doesn't feel ok." If it doesn't feel ok, thank the stone and move on to a new stone and repeat the process until you find a stone that is ready to work with you and wants to be moved. Remember that the spirits of the stones and plants want to work together with humans. The stones are people too, each with their own unique destiny spanning millions of years.

Once you've found a stone, imagine what kind of personality this stone would have if it were a human; just make it up like a child would. To get in touch with your lower self and the Earth element, you must be willing to get silly and not take yourself too seriously.

Once you have the stone in your hand, repeat the process with the a plant. This time ask the plant for one of its leaves, the smallest one on the plant. If it says yes, thank the plant and harvest the leaf by pinching it off, being as gentle as possible.

Smell the stone, and notice how your body feels. Now smell the leaf, and notice how your body feels. Bring the stone to your mouth and taste it. Listen to the sounds in the air, what are the birds saying, what is the wind saying?

Stand in front of the central altar stone where the resins are burning on the charcoal disk.

Hold a square of cloth in your left hand with a string

underneath, the stone and leaf in your right, then hold your hands open and outstretched over the smoke from the altar.

With emotion, ask the stone and the leaf to carry your intentions relating to Earth energy, and thank the stone and plant people for their assistance and friendship. Don't worry about saying exactly the right thing, just feel it, feel what you want to change, what you want to increase inside yourself. You can ask for health, vitality, endurance, stability, security, persistence, and you can offer thanks for what you already have in these areas.

Place the leaf and the stone on the cloth in your left palm and use your right hand to pluck some of your left eyelashes, and place them on top of the leaf and the stone. Tell the Earth elementals that the eyelashes are an offering to them. Thank the ancestors and your guides again for their wisdom and protection.

Take the four corners of the cloth and pull it up around the bundle. Twist it so it has a "head" where the stone and leaf are, and "tails" where the ends of the cloth come out, then triple knot the string directly under the head. With the remaining string length, tie the *prayer tie* to the square protection string hanging above, or to a branch inside the ritual space. Whichever direction represents Earth to you, tie the prayer tie in that direction.

Notice what you feel without judgment. Notice the positive and negative feelings, and let them be. Let the feelings fuel your request to the spirits for healing and help.
Conclude with, *"I give thanks, I give thanks, I give thanks, and so it is."* followed by cracking your knuckles to release and seal the ritual energy.

Take some time to quietly reflect in gratitude, and be present with your body and the Earth.

While I used many words to describe this ritual, once you perform it you will see that it's actually quite simple.

For the strongest effect, perform the ritual on each full Moon and new Moon. On the new Moon, focus on planting your roots into the Earth energy. On the full Moon, focus on gratitude for all the strength and vitality you've received. In between rituals, write in a journal each day and record all of the ways in which you notice more Earth energy coming into your being and your life. Write about any improvements you notice in your vitality and energy levels, improvements in your material, emotional, and mental stability.

This ritual is safe to perform for another person who is in need of help or healing, *as long as you have that person's verbal consent.*

Water Ritual for Forgiveness and Release

This ritual can be done at any time when you feel you have something inside of you that needs to be released, especially when your energy levels or emotions are chaotic and out of balance.

It will purify the Water element inside of you, and point you in the direction of balance. It can be safely performed as often as you need, especially during difficult times or times of grief.

The best location is the East side of a shallow body of water in a secluded place, for example a pond or a stream. If working with a pond or lake, make sure that there is some water flowing out from it so it's not stagnant water. You will need to access the water so make sure it's not too swampy around the edge. The spot needs a stone of any shape near the water that can be used as an altar, preferably about 2 meters from the water.

The best time to perform the ritual is at Moonrise under a full Moon, especially on a Monday (Moonday) in Autumn. Find the spot during the day to make sure it's appropriate. The sky doesn't need to be cloudless, but it should not be raining.

You may be thinking, "Wow, that's very specific!" What I've suggested is the *most beneficial layout and timing*. You don't need to go to the extreme, and in some cases it's better not to. If you are feeling chaotic and need to purify your emotions *right now*, then by all means perform the ritual in a backyard birdbath. When you're ripe for healing, forget the specific details about location and timing and do the ritual.

Don't get stuck in your head! Even if you feel stuck in your head the first time you perform the ritual, as you become more comfortable it will come more from your emotions than your mind.

Materials needed:

- About 20 meters of string.
- A bucket or large bowl.
- Dried chamomile, hops, or comfrey.
- Rosewater.
- Chimes, cymbals, a bell, or a singing bowl.
- For this ritual, burning cypress resin or bark on a charcoal disk is best if you can find it. Otherwise frankincense or camphor are good too.
- 5 beeswax candles.
- Something comfortable to kneel on such as a bolster. or cushion in a plastic bag.

Here's an overview of the ritual

- Gather your materials and find a location with a stone near the water, ideally about 2 meters (6 feet) from the water.
- Offer the ritual to the Moon.
- Dress in blue or teal.
- Use the string to create a circular boundary around the ritual space, touching the water, alter stone in the middle.
- *Open the ritual,* light a candle and chime in each direction and in the centre while giving thanks during the opening.
- Gather water.
- Bless the water with herbs, rosewater, and eyelashes.

- Request blessings and grace from the upper world.
- Breathe the *breath of release.*
- Forgive yourself, forgive others.
- Give thanks to the beneficial spirits who assisted you.
- Offer thanks to the water and return the blessed water to the larger body.
- Reflect and integrate.

Once you've found your location and settled on a time, give away the ritual to the Moon. Dress appropriately for the weather, ideally in blue or teal, and then gather your materials in the space.

In the space, use the string to create a circular boundary on the ground. Ideally the alter stone you've chosen should be in the middle. The edge of the boundary should slightly cross into the body of water, so that it's included inside.

Once everything is in place, *open the ritual,* lighting a candle and sounding your instrument in each of the directions. When thanking Mother Earth, light a candle on the altar stone.

Take your water vessel, and gather water with it, filling it up and thanking the spirit of Water. Bring the water to the altar stone, place some of your eyelashes in the water, then chime over it three times while moving the instrument clockwise.

There are many plant teachers we can ask for help in this process, here I mention three.

- Chamomile is helpful if there is turmoil and chaos which needs to be settled into peace.
- Comfrey helps the healing process of fresh traumas or losses, soothing the pain and knitting the threads back together.
- Hops is powerful in cases of old traumas surfacing which are ready to be forgiven and laid to rest, especially if the trauma relates to sexuality.

Place the plant teacher in the water, and ask it for help. With emotion, tell it exactly what you're struggling with, and ask for kindness, support, and relief. Then add a splash of rosewater to the water.

If the altar is low, use the cushion to kneel. Place your right hand in the water while holding your left hand to the sky, then close your eyes.

Remembering the universal love of the higher spirits, call upon the spirits of the Upper World and request that they bless this water with their grace. Humbly ask them to empower the cleansing power of Water, and to support the plant teachers you are working with. Ask for grace and kindness for yourself. Wait to feel the grace washing down your body, and flowing through your hand into the water.

Relax, remove your hand from the water, and place your right hand on the stone. Close your eyes, and perform the **breath of release**:

- Breathe all of your air out, and hold it out.

- While holding the breath out, contract and then release the muscles of your abdomen, about a second contracted, a second relaxed. Repeat the the cycles of contraction and relaxation for as long as you can.

- When you cannot hold your breath out any longer, take in a deep breath and hold it. Visualize the event or situation which is causing you pain. Think and feel about what is hurting you inside.

- As soon as the pain comes up, repeat the cycle by forcefully breathing all of your air out and then cycling your abdominal muscles between contraction and relaxation, while holding the painful emotions in your belly, mind, and heart.

- Continue this process until you feel the emotion is pouring out of you and into the altar stone.

- If you start to cry that is completely normal and healthy. Allow the tears to flow uninhibited, give into them completely. This is Spirit moving through you and cleansing you.

- Continue until you feel fully emotionally "drained"

Once you've finished, place your right hand in the water and swirl it around 3 times in a clockwise direction. Imagine a time when you've hurt someone, and say to yourself, "I forgive myself for that. I did the best I could, and now I know better." Then take a handful of water, and pour it over the stone. Feel love and gratitude for the plant, stone, and Spirit people who are helping you. Imagine yourself forgiving the past you, and see that they're sorry for the hurt they caused.

Dip your hand in the water again, and remember a time when someone hurt you. Say to them, "I forgive you. You did the best you could with what you knew." Pour the water over the stone, feeling gratitude that you don't need to carry the pain anymore.

Repeat this several times, focusing on forgiving yourself, then focusing on forgiving someone who has hurt you. Continue to do this for as long as it takes to feel neutral.

Once you feel neutral, take a moment for silent reflection and notice how your body feels. Then offer thanks to the beneficial spirits who have helped you in the ceremony.

Finally, pour half of the remaining water on the altar stone, and the rest back into the body of water where it came from. Thank the water for its support, and offer it cleansing and purifying energy in return.

Blow out the five candles, starting at the centre, then the directions starting from the North and going counter-clockwise to the East. Untie the circle, and crack your knuckles to release the energy of the ritual.

Take some time to journal about how you feel after releasing so much stagnant and chaotic energy, writing in a free flowing stream of consciousness, unconcerned with grammar or any other convention.

This ritual is especially valuable in two situation; releasing old trauma which is causing emotional toxicity, and when needing to grieve losing someone close to you. In either case it can be valuable to be surrounded with your family or tribe while performing the ritual. Healing trauma with family members present adds to familial healing, which goes back through the bloodlines and heals the ancestors.

Our trauma doesn't come from nowhere, it has moved down through the generations and you can end it *right now*. In the case of loss, this ritual provides a chance to grieve and heal together, to have loss bring us all together rather than drive us apart. Of course anyone you involve needs to be open to ritual work, and they must be willing to get deep into their emotions on some level, otherwise they will distract from your healing instead of aiding it. If they are not open, it's better that you perform it yourself and then model more harmonious living; you can't rescue anyone.

Fire Ritual for Increasing Auspices of the Sun

In this Fire ritual, you intend to align yourself with the forces of Grandfather Fire and the Sun, and to burn up obstacles within yourself that may block you from receiving their auspices and blessings.

The Sun is the ultimate source of abundance on our planet; you're aligning yourself with the power that builds and increases all things warm, growing, and good. In this ritual, you may also burn your misdeeds from the past to find greater levels of freedom.

You will build a fire, then call in Grandfather Fire to transform this little microcosmic fire into gateway for the macrocosmic element of Fire.

Every tiny piece of matter in the universe that's heavier than helium has passed through the heart of a star, everything heavier than iron was created in a supernova. Your body, and the book that you're reading now passed through a phase of being a star, and then a supernova, so that you could exist.

When you hold a up a dime to the night sky, if you had a telescope powerful enough to see it, you would see at least 100 supernovas within that scope; supernovas that happened billions of years ago, their light just reaching us today.[16]

This is why Fire is the magical element of creation. If there was no Fire, the whole universe would just be dense clouds of helium and nothing else. Keep this image in mind as you go through the ritual. Magic exists, and it created *you*. Out of all

172

of the rituals I share with you, the Fire ritual is the most powerful for increasing tangible beneficial influences for transforming your life and your spiritual practice.

The ideal time to perform the ritual is at noon. Summer and Winter solstice are the best time of year. If you're performing the ritual during the Winter solstice, perform it at midnight instead. Otherwise, Sunday or the new moon are beneficial times.

In chaotic times or during the full moon, you can also perform the ritual to harmonize with the peaceful, strong, and calm aspects of the divine masculine. If you perform the ritual with that intention, wear white during the ritual.

Materials needed:
- The Sunfire rune diagram printed from http://journeying.ca/sunfire and a pushpin.
- Firewood of varied sizes, including kindling, sticks, and logs. The amount depends of size of the ritual.
- A long string for making the boundary, preferably hemp or cotton.
- For each participant:
    - 1/4 cup sesame seeds
    - 1/4 cup brown rice
    - 1/4 cup barley
    - 1/4 cup lentils
    - 1/4 cup organic, wild, or homegrown tobacco (optional, *do not use chemically treated tobacco*)
    - 1 cup water with a splash of rosewater

- 1/2 cup each of camphor and frankincense resin.
- 1/2 pound melted butter (ethically sourced) and a ladle or long handled spoon for pouring.
- 1 jar raw honey.
- Turmeric powder.
- 9 metal or porcelain bowls to hold offerings.
- 12 fresh cut, arms length, straight sticks, cut from the tips of a hardwood tree.
- A simple drawing that represents an obstacle, challenge, or negative influence from your life (past or present).
- A bucket of sand or water for safety, or a fire-extinguisher.
- A traditional fire starting kit such as flint, a knife, and straw, a high quality magnifying glass (preferably quartz), or long matches.

Here's an overview of the ritual

- Offer the ritual to Grandfather Fire and the Sun.
- Gather your materials and find a location on flat open ground. Always be responsible when working with fire, make sure there is nothing flammable nearby and no hanging branches. Respect local fire bans. Make sure firewood is dry and burns readily.
- Built a tipi style fire on bare ground, with a circle of stones surrounding. Ideally the stones should be granite, lava rocks, or other igneous rocks. Place a small handful of camphor with the kindling.
- Dress in yellow.

- Use the string to create a triangular boundary around the ritual space, with the top pointing North (assuming you're in the Northern Hemisphere, otherwise reverse).
- Place the sesame, rice, barley, lentils, tobacco, butter, honey, camphor and frankincense resin, and rosewater infused water each in their own bowl.
- Add about half a teaspoon of turmeric to each bowl and mix it in, with the exception of the water.
- *Open the Ritual.*
- Meditate on the rune.
- Light the fire, welcome Grandfather Fire and the Sun.
- Make offerings and prayers.
- Give thanks, close the ritual, meditate on the dissipating fire.
- Attend to the embers and ashes.

After you've opened the ritual, begin by meditating on the Sunfire rune symbol, feeling gratitude for the Sun and the existence of life on this planet; the fundamental privilege of being alive. Out of the infinite universe, this is the place where your consciousness localized, with this star, on this planet.

Find a comfortable place to sit, and pin the Sunfire rune up in front of you, with the centre at eye level. With your mind and your eyes, focus on the dot in the centre without blinking continuously for 20 minutes. Choosing a spot that isn't too windy, and where your eyes won't be strained by the light will make this easier for you.

While you focus, sitting comfortably, gently bring your mind back to the symbol in front of you whenever it wanders.

Bring your thoughts back to the present moment. Imagine your entire being harmonizing with Fire and the Sun. Once you've aligned yourself with Grandfather Fire and the Sun, begin to call Grandfather Fire in your own words, asking him to come and be a part of your ritual. Ask him to come and bring his warmth and blessings and support. As you do this, light the ritual fire. *If you're not familiar with lighting a fire in general, it would be wise to practice preparing and lighting a few fires before the ritual.*

Once the fire is burning steadily, again ask Grandfather Fire to come and be with you, to bring his primal gifts, and thank him for his warmth and wisdom. Sprinkle frankincense and camphor around the edge of the fire, where it will be slowly warmed and burned.

Sprinkle a small amount of rosewater infused water on the fire with your fingers, ask that all impurities be cleansed, and that all obstacles that would prevent a successful ritual be removed.

Before making an offering, hold the bowl and walk in a circle clockwise around the fire. Visualize the Sun moving through the ritual fire as if it were a gateway; see the Sun entering into the offerings, and into the participants.

Now begin to make the offerings to Grandfather Fire. Each offering has its own property, its own meaning and resonance. For example, turmeric is a plant spirit for cleansing and helping to increase the power of the other offerings.

Slowly pour the melted butter into the centre of the fire with a ladle, as an offering of thanks to Grandfather Fire. Express your gratitude in your own words for whatever Fire has brought into your life and the lives of your family, tribe, and community. Offering butter brings a longer and brighter life to everyone involved in the ritual.

Make the remaining offerings in this order, holding the offering in your hand and contemplating what you're asking for before giving it to the ritual fire.

- Camphor brings clarity and balance of emotions.
- Frankincense brings clarity and balance of mind.
- The sticks are offered in pairs point first; don't mix up their direction. Dip the tips in honey and butter first. They increase alignment with the Sun and remove obstacles to well-being, while bringing you more magnetism. They also feed the macrocosmic spiritual Fire, as offerings of gratitude for all that's already been received.
- Sesame seeds burn up past mistakes and bring self forgiveness.
- Rice is for harmonious alignment in your life and in your self, leading to happiness.
- Barley brings the support of Fire and Solar energy into your intentions and tasks.
- Lentils for increasing strength and health on all levels.
- A spoonful of honey brings more sweetness into your life, and a more harmonious connection with nature, including more support from nature spirits.
- Organic, wild, or homegrown tobacco is the strongest masculine plant spirit on Earth, and supports building positive masculine qualities such as protection, virtue, empowerment, willpower, and directness.

When the offerings are complete, express gratitude to all the spirits, especially to the Sun, Grandfather Fire, the Ancestors, and the Creator. Reaffirm that you are approaching this ritual in a humble way, and ask that the spirits be patient with you as you learn to be with them in a good way. Thank the spirits for supporting your aspirations, and for all the gifts they bring into your life.

After giving thanks, ask the Sun and Grandfather Fire to leave the ritual fire, and to be available in the future. Clap three times, crack your knuckles, and sit in silence as the fire burns out naturally. While the flames diminish to embers, silently reflect on the beneficial and harmonious qualities you've aligned yourself with, and notice how your new alignment affects your thoughts and feelings.

Withdraw all attachment and preference from the outcome of the ritual. Trust that you have put your heart and will forward with healing intentions, and that the universe will continue following its incomprehensible and exquisite dance, bringing grace to all, without exception. Accept that the great power of the universe is beyond your control, while simultaneously knowing that you've aligned yourself with that force of perfect creation and destruction.

After the fire has burned to ashes, save a jar of the ashes for the next Fire ritual. Take some ashes in a bowl and put them in a flowing body of water.

Finally, conclude by pouring the rest of the perfumed water on the ashes, adding more water as needed to extinguish all embers.

Air Ritual for Soaring in the Astral Wind

This ritual is by far the most challenging of the four elemental rituals, and *it is not for everyone*. I recommend that it only be undertaken by those with long term experience with inner work.

The force of the ritual is realized through a week of fasting in an isolated location. You may feel like you're dying, though I assure you that any person in good health will remain healthy. You alone must determine if this ritual is appropriate and safe for you.

With that said, I would never recommend a ritual I haven't performed myself, and I can say that of the four elemental rituals I've shared with you, this one has had the strongest effect on my shamanic path, on my relationship with existence, and on my happiness and contentment in life.

Shamanism is not an easy path. It takes willpower to hold on to a horse's mane while it soars across the plains. During this ritual you will be challenged at many points and in many ways, and by the end you will *transformed.*

During this ritual, you may experience all of the refined qualities of the Air element. Unlike working with plant teachers during a brief ceremony, this ritual gives you the opportunity to deeply align yourself with the harmonious qualities of Air, without the potential chaos and confusion that comes with plant teacher work.

You have the chance to merge with Air, to become one with the astral wind, and to have your armour blown away. In this, you confront your own barriers and resistance, your attachments and compulsions, and your Earth-bound nature. This ritual loosens your roots in their clinging to the Earth, so if you already live with your head in the clouds, perhaps it won't be of the greatest benefit to you.

The element of Air is where we find the purest form of human connection; a place where you can unabashedly connect with your deepest self. The challenge is to find acceptance for yourself at each step, and each misstep.

Physically, the easiest time of year to perform this ritual is summer. The needs of the body are reduced, since it doesn't need to burn as much energy to stay warm. Spiritually, I suggest starting the ritual on a new moon occurring between February 10 and March 15.

For location, I recommend a small cabin far from civilization. You should not be able to hear noise from any human source, nor should you see any light pollution at night, and there should be no likelihood of the ritual being disturbed by anyone. Of lesser importance, there should ideally be no Internet or cell phone service, though a land line is valuable in case of emergency.

This ritual can be performed in a group, or by your self. Each has its own drawbacks and advantages. In a group you can support each other, though being near other people may distract you from your inner process of transformation. If you're the type of person who is uncomfortable being alone, then doing it by yourself may be the most beneficial. If you're a hermit, doing it in a group may help you to open.

While preparing for the ritual, I recommend starting by following Dieta for one to two weeks leading up to the ritual, and then not eating any solid food for one to three days immediately before the ritual. Rather than "fattening up" in the week before the ritual, it's best to ease into it gradually, and let the body adjust to lower caloric intake.

You will not be eating or speaking for one week, giving you the chance to go deep inside yourself and experience countless breakthroughs; a chance to know your true Self in a way you may not have imagined before.

While it may sound daunting, the first 48-72 hours are the most challenging. After that, most people find that the hunger leaves them completely, and then the ritual, the deeper experience, truly begins. If you don't believe you are ready, I recommend not attempting the ritual and continuing to deepen your practice through other avenues. On a personal note, I practised and prepared myself for seven years before I decided I was ready.

Materials needed:

- Beeswax candles, pillar style, enough to burn two at a time, 12 hours a day, for 7 days, as well as candle holders. 10 candles should be enough, depending on their height.
- One piece of white sidewalk chalk. If the cabin is carpeted, 1 roll of white painter's tape or white masking tape.
- Charcoal burning disks for incense, and holder.
- Frankincense, myrrh, and camphor resins.

- Several lighters. Barbecue style lighters with long necks are preferable.
- A home enema kit, and baking soda in a jar.
- A water bottle with an easy to operate lid.
- A chair, meditation bench, yoga mat, or cushions; something you can comfortably sit on to meditate for long periods of time. *I recommend a chair for most people.*
- You may choose to bring a journal, but I suggest that you don't. If you experience great revelations, give them away. Let them be clouds.
- Inspiring books on spirituality and inner exploration that resonate with you. Some suggestions:
  - *The Four Agreements* - Don Miguel Ruiz
  - *The Teachings of Don Juan* - Carlos Castaneda
  - *The Prophet* - Kahlil Gibran
  - *Anastasia* (The Ringing Cedars of Russia series) - Vladimir Megre
  - *Diamond Heart* - A. H. Almaas
  - *The Art of Happiness* - Dalai Lama
  - *The Places that Scare You* - Pema Chodron
  - *Tao Te Ching* - Lao Tzu (Wayne Dyer's meta-translation, *Change Your Thoughts, Change Your Life* is my favourite version)
  - *Become Who You Are* - Alan Watts
  - *What Was Said to the Rose* – Coleman Barks
  - *While reading may be a distraction from the inner unfolding, it can also be supportive in the first three days as the body is adjusting and the mind is agitated.*

182

- The 3 part Air ritual mediation (downloadable for free from http://journeying.ca/meditations/) loaded on a portable music player with headphones. Do not use a smartphone, pick up a used MP3 player if you don't have one.
- White clothing, preferably two or three changes since the ritual is seven days long.
- 1 thumb sized piece of shredded fresh ginger, 1 tablespoon of honey, and 1 fresh lemon, juiced, combined in a 1 litre jar without water and frozen.

The ritual:
Offer the ritual to the stars, and to the infinite loving grace of the Creator.

Move the bed to the middle of the room, and place two nightstands beside it, then place your meditation chair/bench/cushions in front of the foot of the bed. Using chalk or tape, create a six pointed star enclosing the bed, the nightstands, and the meditation area, representing the living union of your human soul with the Creator.

Place a candle on each nightstand in its holder. Place the incense burner on the right side, and your water bottle and any books on the left.

Light the candles, being mindful of fire safety. If you have performed the Fire ritual, you may welcome Grandfather Fire and the Sun to enter into the candles and support the ritual. Start a charcoal disk in the holder, then place a small amount of frankincense, myrrh, and camphor on the charcoal.

Open the ritual.

Sitting in your meditation area, offer these words:
"I offer these seven days of austerity of food and words to the eternally sustaining and silent Creator, to the Source of the manifest and unmanifest universe. I surrender my illusions of doership, of separate sense of self, and of control to the dance of the Great Mystery, which animates everything. I release myself into your breeze. I accept that I am but a witness and that all of this activity arises from the Infinite. I accept that I am a grain of pollen floating on your breath. *I thank you, thank you, thank you, for this chance to be incarnated, to be witness, to experience the many facets of being.*"

From this point on, maintain complete silence and consume no calories until the ritual has ended at sunset on day seven. This is a vow of austerity made by your soul to the universal Soul.

After the ritual is open, begin the Air ritual meditation by sitting in a meditative position, relaxed with a straight spine, and then listen to the guided meditation.

After the guided meditation, take an hour or two to walk around, slowly and mindfully, wherever the body goes. Be aware of each muscle movement, each sensation in the body, each thought and emotion. Without judgment, see how simply observing and detaching from these phenomena allows them to pass quickly and effortlessly.

Remember that you are not the doer; not the mover or the body, not the thinker or the thoughts, not the feeler or the emotions.

184

All of this arises from wholeness, arises from the Source. You are the observer; you observe. You are the empty sky that the clouds pass through, the river full of bubbles.

You may experience desires; accept them as they pass through. The body will have needs, observe them as they arise. Observe the interactions between body, mind, and emotion, all separate from you, the observer. The body wants to eat, the emotions want to talk, the mind wants to fixate. Observe how they are each affected by austerity. **This is the fundamental practice of the Air ritual.**

After walking, return to the ritual space and perform an enema using body temperature water and 1 level tablespoon of baking soda per litre of water. Follow the directions on the kit. Because the movement of the intestines (peristalsis) stops while fasting, the body can have a harder time eliminating toxins. Enemas help to remove the toxins that would otherwise accumulate in the body, which could cause feelings of sickness or heaviness. Baking soda is highly alkaline and makes the process easier.

After the cleansing: tonglen meditation, reading, or resting the body may arise. Observe. Be the sky and accept the clouds – physical discomfort; negative emotions; mental agitation – which pass through, without judgment. If judgment arises, do not judge the judgment.

This completes the first day.

A schedule for the next six days follows:
- Begin each day by waking at 4am, stretching the body, drinking water, washing the body and brushing the teeth. Whenever needed throughout, the burning of candles and incense arises.

- Begin the guided Air ritual meditation at 5am.

- Walk mindfully, while observing all internal and external phenomena.

- Return to the ritual space, allowing action and non-action to arise, being present with existence in all its facets.

- At some point each day, it is valuable to perform an enema with baking soda to cleanse the body, emotions, and mind.

It is also valuable to meditate if the body is able to sit; eventually the meditation arises constantly and effortlessly, as the observer becomes more distanced from the body, emotions, and mind.

When meditation arises, observe energy moving through the being:
With each inhalation, the mind focuses on the profound grace of the universe pouring in through the top of the head, and then settling into the heart. On each exhalation, the grace goes out to all beings as loving kindness.
The energy can also move in reverse:
On each inhalation, the mind notices loving kindness flowing into the heart, igniting the heart and fanning it as if it were

an ember. Then on the exhalation, flowing out of the top of the head, as gratitude for all existence.

As you observe all of this taking place, you will find yourself becoming lighter and lighter. You will find yourself accepting both joy and sorrow as equals; you will come to abide in the Spirit of the Truth. The transformation takes place gradually, through stillness, observation, and unconditional acceptance.

At sunset on the seventh day, add warm water to the jar of ginger, honey, and lemon juice. Mix it up, offer it to the spirits with gratitude, and have a sip. Drink it very slowly, over several hours.

The closing of this ritual must be guided by Spirit, and so I leave it to Spirit to guide. You will know what to do; you will understand that grace arises from non-action.

If for any reason at all the ritual must end early, which I *highly recommend against*, acknowledge to the spirits that the vow of seven days of austerity is being broken, and thank them for all you experienced for as long as it lasted. Do not make excuses and do not apologize, regardless of the reason. Acknowledge, accept, and express gratitude.

In the days following the ritual, continue to take quiet time and eat minimally; return to the Earth slowly, building a bridge from Heaven down to Earth. Give the body, emotions, mind, and soul (you) a chance to knit back together slowly, to create a foundation for a new and more harmonious relationship going forward.

Final words

I am deeply honoured to hold space for this alchemy of the soul, and I am inspired by the courageous warriors of light who are engaging with this sacred healing modality. Blessed journey to you.

May the sons and daughters of Abraham
look at the indigenous peoples of this Earth,
the ones who hold the old ways sacred,
with kindness and respect.
Acknowledging the genocide which has swept the Earth,
may they find acceptance and forgiveness;
may the younger brother find a good way.

I call upon the First Peoples of this Earth,
I call upon my Táltos ancestors;
I'm listening to you, and I thank you for guiding us all in a
good way, and for bringing light and justice to
this dark time we are living in;
thank you for warming us
while we await the break of day.

Thank you Creator for all you have given all.
Thank you plant teachers, animal teachers, stone
teachers, and all my relations, who guide
the heart of humanity.

Thank you all humans who humbly live in a good way.
I give thanks, I give thanks, I give thanks,
and so it is.
With love and gratitude,
Ankhara

References and Further Reading

1: See more quotes at http://ayahuasca.info

2: For more information on the neurochemistry involved see: *The Scientific Investigation of Ayahuasca* , by Mckenna DJ, Callaway JC, Grob CS.

https://www.erowid.org/chemicals/ayahuasca/ayahuasca_journal3.shtml

3: See *Ayahuasca and Cancer Treatment*, Eduardo E Schenberg 2013.

http://smo.sagepub.com/content/1/2050312113508389.abstract and *Phytochemistry* 66 (13): 1581–92, Jahaniani, F; Ebrahimi, SA; Rahbar-Roshandel, N; Mahmoudian, M (July 2005).

4: On false personality; A H Almaas, Diamond Heart Book III, Pg. 43, http://ahalmaas.com/glossary/personality/4040

5: See Carl Jung's theories on *Puer aeternus*

https://en.wikipedia.org/wiki/Puer_aeternus#The_puer_in_Jungian_psychology

6: See the works of psychologist Harville Hendricks

7: Learn more about confabulation and false memories: Kring, A. M., Johnson, S. L., Davison, G. C., & Neale, J. M. (2010) *Abnormal psychology*

8: See the works of Stanislav Grof

9: http://www.maps.org/news-letters/v21n1/v21n1-21to22.pdf

10: On merging and symbiotic union: Diamond Heart Book I,

Pg. 7, http://www.ahalmaas.com/glossary/mother/3831

11: Lee N. Robins PhD, John E. Helzer MD, Michie

Hesselbrock MSW and Eric Wish PhD (1977) *Vietnam*

Veterans Three Years after Vietnam: How Our Study

Changed Our View of Heroin & Johann Hari (2015)

Chasing The Scream: The First and Last Days of the War on

Drugs

12: Map and list of indigenous use: http://bit.ly/indigenous-ayahuasca

13: See *Vegetalismo - Shamanism Among the Mestizo*

Population of the Peruvian Amazon

14: John Hawks, Keith Hunley, Sang-Hee Lee, and Milford

Wolpoff, *Population Bottlenecks and Pleistocene Human*

Evolution http://mbe.oxfordjournals.org/content/17/1/2.long

15: Marshall Sahlins "original affluent society" theory. See

also *Ishmael* and *The Story of B* by Daniel Quinn

16: Lawrence M. Krauss

https://en.wikipedia.org/wiki/Lawrence_M._Krauss

Acknowledgements

Thank you to my human teachers, for all the the wisdom, patience, and kindness you've taught me. Thank you Grandmother Illona, Helen, Juan, Lena, Dov, Stan, Kush, and the many fellow travellers on this path who have shared your wisdom with me.

Thank you to Despina, Johnny, Justin, Kai, Karl, Lauren, Laurie, Laynah, Lei Chandra, Martina, Nimisha, Saeed, Shane, Siobahn, and Stina for your sagely wisdom and feedback on AMoR. Your contributions have added so much clarity, readability, and depth the this work, for I am forever grateful to call you family.

Thank you to my family and my tribe, for all of your love, support, and encouragement in preserving and deepening our traditions.

Dedication

This work is dedicated to the descendants; I pray that you inherit a world of harmony and beauty, and to the indigenous people of the Earth; may you receive the dignity and respect you deserve.

Legalities

What I've shared with you in this book originates in ancient traditions, and is tempered by modern understandings. I have done my best to transmit this wisdom in alignment, integrity, and continuity with those traditions.

However, I cannot take responsibility for any actions you choose to take based on these ideas, nor can I take responsibility for how you may react. I am not a medical professional, and I share these practices with you purely as information to be pondered, not as advice of any kind, and I leave it to you to do with as you see fit. Given statements made by the United Nations, I believe that everything described in this book is fully protected by international laws relating to religious freedom, but local laws and enforcement vary from place to place.

While I have endeavoured to share well researched and high quality information with you, if you notice something which you believe to be factually incorrect, please contact me so that I may correct it. I am not perfect, not all knowing, just another traveller on the path, and I appreciate any information or corrections that you have to share with me.

All quotations and meta-translations are used under public domain, or fair use. If you own the rights to any content included or referenced in this book and believe it was incorrectly used, please contact ankhara@journeying.ca to have it it credited, edited, or removed.

Copyright Information

Made in the USA
San Bernardino, CA
14 March 2017